The Harmful Effects of Prejudice and Discrimination

Author: Shabbir H M Tankiwala

Who created whom? Humans created God a figment of our imagination or god created human beings.

Is god real or is it just a myth? Are we humans deliberately made to believe by none other than our own creators to believe that there exist a "Divine (Super Natural) Power" (whom we call/believe as "God"), the God who has an unprecedented power and control over the destiny of each of the human. Many intellectuals surmise that maybe our creators, perhaps, may have embedded such fearful thoughts in the mind of us (humans) and must have done so, with an intention to create a fear psycho in the mind of mankind, so that we (humans) remain within our limits and disciplined and do not indulge in any kind nefarious activity.

People throughout history have created a god to meet their own needs and circumstances. But, the REAL God of the Universe cannot be the creation of mere man's logic and mental comprehension.

We are not "God," but our desire to be such takes us to madness.

However, The findings of the scientific community and the archaeologist over the years of their intense research studies have discovered and have establish the fact, which suggest, apparently we humans have been created by the extra-terrestrial, that means we humans have been created by the "Alien" (Ancient Alien) or to say the "UFO."

Even Though it's difficult to ascertain as to, how true is this study done by the scientific community indicating that we humans are creation of Alien, as there still lies many questions and lingering doubts in the minds of us all, hence, it will always be difficult to conclusively come to any conclusion about the fact, as in, from, where and how have we "Humans" come into existence on this Planet earth? Also there are still many staunch sceptics who are ever so adamant and not willing to accept the fact of any kind of evolution theory and to believe the scientific findings about the creation of humans, they strongly argue that we the humans are creation of one and only and that's the so-called "Almighty' God."

However it is an established fact that this planet of ours (Earth) have been visited in the past by the extra-terrestrial, hence, it seems highly likely that we humans may have been created by them the "extra-terrestrial elements" called Ancient Aliens.

The scientific discovery, they believe, the so-called 97% non-coding sequence in human DNA is no less than genetic code of extra-terrestrial life forms.

So if we are to assume that we humans have been the creation of the extra-terrestrial, so are we also to assume that our own creators may have been having grave fundamental differences among themselves and that perhaps may have been the reason that our creators own difference of opinions and bitter rivalry among them and because of their clash of ego, hence in frustration and duress our creators may have planned and plotted the division amongst we humans, it gives us reasons to assume, that our creators must have promoted various religious belief solely for the purpose of creating wedge among we humans, are the creators of "humans" themselves responsible to have cause distrust and discord among we humans? And various "Ethnic Communities, Races and Religions" formed act as a catalyst in dividing us "we the people."

Whatever may be true, the fact remains that we humans for ages have been divided among ourselves, we humans like to dislike each other, whether or not if God's a myth or real.

Many among us "humans" waste invaluable time of ours in our life time, thinking about God, talking about God, discussing about God, most of the people we talk too, they use the word "God" as many time as they can during the course of the conversation, these people start conversation with the name of

"God" and ends the conversation with the name of "God." Most of the people spends unprecedented amount of their time in their life time, thinking, talking, reading and understanding about "God" so much time of theirs in their life time is invested in God that they fail to understand their own-selves.

In good times and in bad times, in happiness and in sorrow, in glum and glory, people think of "God" and talk of only "God."

Chapter 1

Believe in yourself only if you are convince about your own decision making ability, which means if you are convince that you've Good instinct or if you are convince that you are unlikely to make any mistakes, please have no illusion in your mind about your own intelligence and knowledge, else, if you have any doubt in your mind about your own instinct don't ever take a risk of believing in yourself or trusting yourself because more often than not the bitter enemy of ours is none other than we our own-self, our mind is our best friend and our worst enemy. This paradox it doesn't even tell us which level of functionality our memory is operating at when we experience these personifications.

Never interrupt your enemy when he/she is making mistake.

The smart person learns from his/her own mistake but the smarter/smartest learns from others mistakes.

Your worst enemy cannot harm you as much as your own unguarded thoughts.

Mismanagement of economy + Bad economic policy = inflation = corruption = crime = to civilian unrest.

People often misunderstand the notion of independent event. The past events have no influence on future outcome. Realistically the odds of winning substantial amount of money without losing significant amount are very low.

Believe in helping your own-self, every one of us should be determine to strive to empower our-selves, Don't ever get into the habit of surviving on others help or support, shun the habit of accepting external help or aid, learn not to survive on the mercy and charity of governments and charitable trust.

My favourite politician and President of India, "Mr Pranab Mukherjee" once said "The government is not a charity shop, populist anarchy cannot be substitute for governance" He also said, " Elections doesn't give any person the licence to flirt with illusions.

Many politicians and many governments across the globe simply to keep their political constituency in good humour and to win favours of particular "Race, linguistic minority/majority or Religious groups" to win elections, this lot of politicians brazenly dole out goodies and freebies to particular section of society, they generously open the government coffers.

There are several countries with perfect examples, the countries such as "Japan, Singapore, Hong Kong and South-Korea are all thriving economies despite the fact that these countries have no significant amount of natural resources and on the other side there are many countries in Africa and South America whom the "Nature" has blessed them abundantly with rich natural resources like minerals and hydrocarbons, these countries in Africa and South America despite having immense natural resources and manpower, yet, these country's economies are faltering and large section of its population are living in desperate poverty.

So, among many reasons, bi-polar division between affluent class and underclass is also a major factor that causes civilian unrest and disharmony in civil society.

If everyone in this world becomes "Cash Rich," will the hatred among people based on "Ethnicity, Race, Religion and Region" dissipate?

The answer is "NO," bickering and discrimination among humans is as old as is recorded history, humans will always have some reason or the other to quarrel and rant among themselves.

Now Let us find answers for some of the most pressing questions.

Why has there never been complete harmony among humans, ever since we've come into existence?

Why do humans have the sordid history of fighting bloody wars and battles, which have resulted in countless deaths?

Why is there so much hate crimes, in civil society?

Why in most civil societies "particularly" the women's are discriminated?

Why is there a need for countries to build and possess weapons of mass destruction?

Why do countries spend unprecedented amount of money on combative military forces?

Well, for all these above raised questions, there are more answers than there are questions and if the above raised issues are crux for discontent in civil society than there are also many solutions as well.

So than, why have we so far never amicably sorted out these contentious issues and have made this world safe and better place to leave in?

The fact is that, the problems are more fundamental, basically we humans are simply not interested in resolving issues, human's mind set is puzzle and they like to keep burning issues alive, because for many selfish individuals the misery of others are good business opportunity and to capture political power as well as there are many selfish who rejoice themselves when they observes the plight and agony of others.

But, now to find out more about these, The real fundamental problem of not getting issues resolve, and ever increasing social division among humans on basis of "Race, Religion and Region" is the weak, selfish or astute" Political leadership.

At our home our parents are our leaders, in schools and universities our head teachers are our leaders at work our managers are our leaders and on large scale at national level it's the politicians are our leaders, The person whosoever and where so ever, when gets an opportunity to lead the people also has the onus on them to give the right guidance and bring unity and lead its followers to peace and harmony, more important is that the leaders should practice what they preach.

But more often the person who's made a leader is often found to be playing destructive role, the leaders be it business or political leaders they themselves often subtly sabotage the peace and harmony in civil society by dividing people on racial and religious line.

The person who gets an opportunity of playing a leadership role, himself/ herself fails to live up to the expectation.

Discussing the ideas you have with others is "No" good, because the world is full of people who have loads of ideas, the real fruit is in executing the ideas you have, The benefit lies in executing your thoughts and ideas, and not merely discussing and debating with others.

Not "Contemplation" but Implementation is what matters most.

Most often a goal of keeping your head above water, end up sinking you, so the purpose of our life should be not merely surviving but to strive and thrive.

Chapter 2

Let us discuss,

Racism vs Prejudice

Mussolini invented the term totalitarianism, but its roots go back to the very dawn of history.

Indeed, ideas like eugenics and euthanasia go back to the very beginning of intellectual thought.

From the world of ancient India to the ideas of Plato, the concept of human inequality is as old as history.

The same can be said for the concept of respect for nature and nature's law.

Prejudice is a negative feeling you have over an entire group of people, often an ethnic group or racial group.

Racism is a kind of prejudice, where you think one "race" is superior and all the others are inferior, it has to do more to do with physical traits than anything else.

Racism can be limited to belief, though you can act with racism, while prejudice is nearly always an action (or omission of action), so you can be racist without showing prejudice, but if you are prejudiced, there is nearly, there is always an under-lying belief such as racism, sexism, anti-gay bias, and so one prejudice is a more general term in that it means, to judge without evidence based on some belief.

Prejudice implies jumping to conclusion or letting post experiences or perceived characteristics of a group affect your judgement and how you treat individuals, for instance, if you were robbed in the past, it would be prejudice to assume all people of the same group robs others.

Prejudice can also be refer to unfounded beliefs and may include "any unreasonable attitude that is unusually resistant to rotational influence."

Racism means to believe particular "race" is better,

A related term Discrimination and that is an unequal treatment, while not discrimination is a type of racism, and while not all racism is discrimination, they are related to one another and overlap, Discrimination implies having authority or power to make decisions, so, while badmouthing people of particular "race" moving into your neighbourhood would be racist, actually preventing them from doing so, discrimination based on racism.

Racial prejudice is an insidious moral and social disease affecting peoples and populations all over the world. It is diagnosed by the cataloguing of its various symptoms and manifestations which include fear, intolerance, separation, segregation, discrimination and hatred. While all these symptoms of racial prejudice may be manifest, the single underlying cause of racial prejudice is ignorance. Historically a "race" of people is defined as a population with distinguishable biological features.

People are still unclear as to just what racism is. Many people confuse racism with prejudice. Prejudice is the forming of an unfavourable opinion based on colour, gender, sexual orientation, etc. with no actual knowledge or experience of the person or people specifically. Racism is where one believes that there is a difference in races, and that one is superior to others (usually their own). Other races are viewed upon with hate or intolerance.

Why is it that people cannot rationally discuss and help one another understand just what it is that they are doing or perceiving? Who truly has zero effect on our lives, but we cannot spend hours asking why people are so prejudiced against Muslims or why it is that racism is overlooked daily from people who happen to not be famous? Why, we cannot talk about ourselves or the fact that racism still lurks in entire communities within our country?

A Sunni terrorist detonates a bomb at a crowded Shiite shrine in Iraq. Political anti-Semitism is on the rise in the Russian Federation, even though most of its Jews have long-since emigrated. Millions of Central Africans have died because of the long-standing enmity between the Tutsi and Hutu peoples.

Prejudice is present in almost every community, but its levels and loci are constantly shifting. If Germany engineered the worst genocide in recorded history in the 1940s, it is a relatively tolerant place today. Lebanon, once noted for its cosmopolitanism, is much more divided now. What are the drivers of prejudice and tolerance? What makes them wax and wane?

Put any one country or region under a microscope and you'll quickly discern the uniquely local qualities of its hatreds. The Middle East has long been divided along religious and ethnic lines. The breakup of the former Soviet Union awakened dormant nationalist aspirations in places like Georgia and Chechnya. Cambodia and Thailand suffer from stark economic divides and are also traditional enemies.

Still, it's just as important to step back and look at the bigger picture. What are the key social, demographic and economic factors underlying prejudice? What effect does prejudice have on the wealth and happiness of nations?

First and foremost, prejudice is associated with economic backwardness. With a few notable exceptions, it clusters most heavily in places that are rife with substantial economic, political, and cultural stress. Prejudiced countries also tend to be poorer and less developed. It is hard to say what causes what – whether prejudice holds development back or retarded development engenders prejudice – but the connection is clear.

The bottom line? Prejudice is not just morally reprehensible, it's economically punishing as well.

When prejudice occurs, stereotyping and discrimination may also result. In many cases, prejudices are based upon stereotypes. A stereotype is a simplified assumption about a group based on prior assumptions. Stereotypes can be both positive ("women are warm and nurturing") or negative ("teenagers are lazy"). Stereotypes can lead to faulty beliefs, but they can also result in both prejudice and discrimination.

By stereotyping we infer that a person has a whole range of characteristics and abilities that we assume all members of that group have. Stereotypes lead to social categorization, which is one of the reasons for prejudice attitudes (i.e. "them" and "us" mentality) which leads to in-groups and out-groups.

Victims of prejudice, or those who perceive they are, may have difficulty focusing on tasks and making clear decisions, an effect which can linger after the incident. Researchers at the University of Toronto Scarborough studied individuals' reactions to negative stereotyping, and found that after being placed in a situation where they were victims of prejudice, many people found it hard to concentrate or were even aggressive. Since an individual's ability to turn his full attention to a task is impaired, a victim of prejudice is placed at a disadvantage in academic environments.

Prejudice excludes people in many ways. For example, an employer might be prejudiced against a certain ethnic group, and would therefore be less likely to accept job applications from members of that group and would look more favourably on candidates from another ethnicity. An individual who suffers from a mental health problem might find that she is excluded from certain social activities, since others may perceive her as dangerous, and may not receive support from medical services.

Prejudice and discrimination may lead to physical, sexual, emotional, and/or mental abuse. Being the victim of prejudice or discrimination can negatively impact a person's emotional well-being and sense of self, especially if they experience prejudice or discrimination on an ongoing basis due to an intrinsic characteristic of who they are as a person. People who are prejudged or discriminated against may develop physical or mental health problems as a result of the discriminatory actions of others.

A prejudiced person may not act on their attitude. Therefore, someone can be prejudiced towards a certain group but not discriminative against them. Also, prejudice includes all three components of an attitude (affective, behavioural and effective), whereas discrimination just involves behaviour.

Over a period of time, a victim of constant prejudice might begin to believe that he deserves the abuse or problems he/she has encountered, and that prejudiced individuals are right to treat him in such a way. An individual who believes negative comments about his own group is suffering from self-stigma, as described by the Centre for Addiction and Mental Health website. This belief can, in turn, lead to further problems, as the individual is likely to suffer from poor self-esteem and may even fall into depression.

An extreme example of prejudice and discrimination would be the Nazi's mass murder of Jews in the Second World War, or the killings of Catholics by Protestants and Protestants by Catholics or the Sunni Muslims killing Shiite Muslims.

Article title "**Consequence of Prejudice**" describes: "Like the wide variety of prejudices that exist in societies around the world, the consequences of the prejudices and the behaviour influenced by them are similarly varied. Prejudice affects the everyday lives of millions of people across the globe. Prejudice held by individuals unnaturally forces on others who are targets of their prejudice a false social status that strongly influences who they are, what they think, and even the actions they take. Prejudice shapes what the targets of prejudice think about the world and life in general, about the people around them, and how they feel about themselves. Importantly, prejudice greatly influences what people expect from the future and how they feel about their chances for self-improvement, referred to as their life chances. All of these considerations define their very identity as individuals.

People acting out their prejudices causes domestic violence, crime, death, and the loss of billions of dollars in lost productivity, property loss, and expense to society, such as cost of court trials and social services provided to victims including psychological counselling, in dealing with dysfunctional (abnormal behaviour) elements of society. Other prejudicial behaviour, such as male teachers favouring calling on male students in a classroom, may be more subtle (less obvious). But its effect can be just as broad-sweeping as the more violent consequences of prejudice. Opportunities in life are lost and personal relationships damaged when people act upon their prejudice. When not acknowledged and confronted, prejudice negatively impacts the lives not only of the victims, but of those holding the prejudice.

Prejudice can impose very dramatic barriers or invisible barriers on individuals. For example, in the United States, many children are raised with certain beliefs, one being the American Dream. The children are taught if they apply themselves and work hard enough and set their sights on what they want most, they can achieve it by persistence. They are not taught about certain social barriers, such as racial or gender discrimination in hiring or in job promotions, that may present themselves throughout their lives that counter the progress made by solid work habits."....

Since multiple prejudices are present throughout society in a complex way, at minimum, the consequences of prejudice are always present in subtle, if not more obvious, ways. For example, because people are largely aware of the prejudices held by others toward them, the prejudice has a self-fulfilling effect. This means people behave the way others expect them to behave. Similarly, people holding a prejudice treat others differently based on how the person with prejudices expects the others to behave or how the person with prejudices wants the others to behave. These behavioural expectations are often based on stereotypes. Stereotypes are an oversimplified prejudgment of others using physical or behavioural characteristics, usually exaggerated, that supposedly apply to every member of that group. In addition, people behave differently from person to person when interacting with others, depending on whether they expect hostility from others either in attitude or in action. Studies have shown that a person targeted by stereotype expectations held by others may end up behaving as the stereotype. More generally, a person is likely to behave as the other person expects him to behave. All of these behaviours mean that prejudice, or anticipated prejudices, affect everyday interactions with almost everyone a person comes in contact with.

Consequences of everyday prejudice go beyond simply shaping relationships between people. People are relentlessly assaulted by value judgments based on skin colour, social class, gender, religious affiliation, political views, and so on. Such constant exposure to ridicule and discrimination leads to a lowered self-esteem. Those subjected to such prejudice become unsure where they belong in society. They develop hatred and anger directed both outwardly at those holding prejudices against them and inwardly for having the supposed traits that attract such prejudices. Such prejudices are destructive of individuals and society. But they extract a hidden cost as well by prohibiting individuals from living up to their true potential.

Very small but harmful prejudicial actions can create barriers for entire populations, such as women or minorities, seeking to enjoy the benefits of participating in mainstream society. Often these actions are unintentional, caused by prejudices a person is little aware he has. However, many times they are intentional acts meant to degrade another person considered inferior. It is sometimes difficult to determine if an act is unintended and simply insensitive or meant as intentional hostility. Regardless of intentions, the consequence of action is often the same. Many times the person who is the target of such prejudicial actions is placed in difficult situations. Any protest he or she might make of such prejudicial actions would give the appearance of oversensitivity and possibly incite further reaction from the initiator. For example, a woman may be placed in an awkward situation when she is congratulated for offering a solution to a technical engineering problem as if such an idea would not be normally expected of a woman.

The person targeted by prejudicial actions is not the only person affected. Prejudice affects the behaviour of the person holding the prejudice as well. That person may harbour anxieties or anger, or alter his normal activity because of the prejudice he feels for someone else. Such feelings of prejudice can lead to alcohol and substance abuse just as for people who are the targets of prejudice.

Fascism and Racism

"Fascism is an open terrorist dictatorship of the most reactionary, the most chauvinistic, the most imperialistic elements of the financial capital... Fascism is neither the government beyond classes nor the government of the petty bourgeois or the lumpen-proletariat over the financial capital. Fascism is the government of the financial capital itself. It is an organized massacre of the working class and the revolutionary slice of peasantry and intelligentsia. Fascism in its foreign policy is the most brutal kind of chauvinism, which cultivates zoological hatred against other peoples."

The world in recent memory witness and experience the worst form of "Fascism and Racism" was in the twentieth century after the end of "world war 1," and The Two Kingpin and the names of these two gentlemen who led the world into the "2nd world war" are the "Italian Mr Benito Mussolini" the founder leader of Italy's "National Fascist Party" and other the most notorious "German NAZI leader Adolf Hitler."

While Mussolini, who in his early part of his life was a devout socialist but after the "world war 1" he turned into an authoritarian and became a Fascist movement leader and thereby became supreme leader of Italy and he ruled Italy for well over two decades, while Mussolini was an atheist.

Hitler was more of a racist. But, however it has been observed by some political analyst according to them "Hitler per se was not even racist, he had sly motives, he actually was more of an ambitious power hungry flamboyant man. Hitler's motives were destructive. Hitler was a Trojan horse designed to destroy Germany's national, cultural and racial pretensions."

Fascism was born in Italy and subsequently spread across Europe wherein several movements which took influence from it.

The most striking difference is the racialist and anti-Semitic ideology present in Nazism but not the other ideologies.

Fascism was founded on the principle of Nationalist unity, against the Divisionist class war ideology of socialism and communism. Thus the majority of regimes viewed racialism as counterproductive.

Italian fascism was expansion in its desires, The "National Fascist Party" wanted to create a **New Roman Empire** and Nazi Germany objective was to expand its border.

Countries such as "Spain and Portugal" remain neutral in world-war 2.

Hitler and the Nazi also thought people could be divided into different "Races" and that there was a struggle going on between these different Races. According to Nazi's "Aryan Race" was best and strongest race, and the Jews were of another "race" in fact so inferior that they were not considered to be "People" by the Nazi's.

Whenever a study of the Nazis is undertaken, there is one burning question that emerges;

How could a cultured nation, at the heart of Europe, be responsible for acts so horrible, so inhuman?

Did Hitler invented hatred of Jews? No, Hitler built on and used anti-Semitic ideas that already existed.

Hitler was an Austrian and he grew up in Vienna where the mayor was extremely anti-Semitic and where hatred against Jews was widespread.

Hitler spread his beliefs in Racial "Purity" and in superiority of "Germanic Race" – what he called an Aryan "Master" Race," he pronounced that his Race must remain pure in order to one day take over the world, for Hitler, the ideal "Aryan" was blond, blue eyed and tall.

Now very interesting, a million dollar question.

Was Adolf Hitler either by his own definition of "Aryan Race" or biologically a "True" Aryan?

The billion dollar answer to the million dollar question is,

No, Adolf Hitler "neither by his own definition of "Aryan Race" nor biologically was an Aryan, Hitler himself had a strong Jewish connect, Hitler's "DNA" was at least 25% Jewish and wasn't an "Aryan."

After nearly Four long decades of turbulent and political turmoil, in the mid 1940's Europe was trying to recover from the massive loss of lives and major decimation and devastation caused to all its major towns and cities, Europe embrace liberalism and secularism and drafted secular and freedom to all "constitution."

But thousands of miles away from Europe in the southern most African country, yes, we are talking about "South-Africa," in the year 1948 a draconian "Law" was being drafted. The ruling "National Party" of South-Africa made drastic changes in amending its "Constitution."

Apartheid (apart-hood), word meaning "state of apart" literally "apart-hood) was a system of racial segregation in South-Africa enforced through legislation by the National Party Government, The ruling party of South Africa from 1948 to 1994.

South African apartheid with enactment of apartheid Law in 1948, racist discrimination was institutionalised, Race Laws touched every aspect of life, including prohibition of marriage between "Non-whites and Whites" and the sanctioning of "white only" jobs.

In 1950, the Population Registration Act required that South-Africans be racially classified into one of three categories; White, Black (African) or Coloured (mixed descent) the coloured category included major subgroups of Indians and Asians.

The greatest and the most powerful country in the world "United States of America" as well have its own history of grave Racial discrimination, first the "Native American" than the "Black Africans" slaves.

Millions of natives occupied the area now called the United States prior to the colonial era. In an effort to obtain much of the North American as territory of the United States, a long series of wars, massacres, forced displacement, restriction of food rights and the imposition of treaties, land was taken and numerous hardships imposed. Ideologies justifying the context included stereotypes of Natives Americans as "merciless Indian savages" and the quasi-religious doctrine of manifest destiny which asserted divine blessing for U.S. conquest of all lands of the Atlantic seaboard to the Pacific.

Once their territories were incorporated into the United States, many surviving Native Americans were relegated to reservations--constituting just 4% of U.S. territory, and the treaties signed with them violated. Tens of thousands of them were forced to attend a residential school system which sought to re-educate them in white settler American values, culture and economy.

Slavery in the United States began soon after English colonists first settled Virginia and lasted until the passage of the Thirteenth Amendment to the United States Constitution in 1865. By the 18th century, court rulings established the racial basis of the American version of slavery to apply chiefly to Black Africans and people of African descent, and occasionally to Native Americans. The 19th century saw a hardening of institutionalized racism and legal discrimination against citizens of African descent in the United States. Although technically able to vote, poll taxes, acts of terror (often perpetuated by groups such as the KKK), and discriminatory laws kept black Americans disenfranchised particularly in the South.

Racism in the United States was worse during this time than at any period before or since. Segregation, racial discrimination, and expressions of white supremacy all increased. So did anti-black violence, including lynching and race riots.

In modern era of 21st century we have read about and have seen images of the most cruellest of inhuman activity particularly in most of the Muslim dominated countries in west-Asia and in North-Africa. The brutal and venomous Sunni-Muslim jihadist terrorist groups such as BoKo-Haram and Al-Shabaab and most severe and brutal jihadist group of all the ISIS (Islamic State of Iraq & al-Sham) these ferocious jihadist (Islamic Holy-warrior) groups staunchly believes in enslaving young women and girls and sexually exploiting them, however we should find out few details about past history as well of hatred crimes and slavery, here what reminds me is the history of brutal atrocities that was so remorselessly unleashed on Irish white-women; **Article titles "The Irish Slave Trade – The Forgotten "White Slaves"** describes the most ugliest form of discrimination of Irish women; *"They came as slaves; vast human cargo transported on tall British ships bound for the Americas. They were shipped by the hundreds of thousands and included men, women, and even the youngest of children.*
Whenever they rebelled or even disobeyed an order, they were punished in the harshest ways. Slave owners would hang their human property by their hands and set their hands or feet on fire as one form of punishment. They were burned alive and had their heads placed on pikes in the marketplace as a warning to other captives.
We don't really need to go through all of the gory details, do we? We know all too well the atrocities of the African slave trade.
But, are we talking about African slavery? King James II and Charles I also led a continued effort to enslave the Irish. Britain's famed Oliver Cromwell furthered this practice of dehumanizing one's next door neighbour.

The Irish slave trade began when James II sold 30,000 Irish prisoners as slaves to the New World. His Proclamation of 1625 required Irish political prisoners be sent overseas and sold to English settlers in the West Indies. By the mid 1600s, the Irish were the main slaves sold to Antigua and Montserrat. At that time, 70% of the total population of Montserrat were Irish slaves.

Ireland quickly became the biggest source of human livestock for English merchants. The majority of the early slaves to the New World were actually white.

From 1641 to 1652, over 500,000 Irish were killed by the English and another 300,000 were sold as slaves. Ireland's population fell from about 1,500,000 to 600,000 in one single decade. Families were ripped apart as the British did not allow Irish dads to take their wives and children with them across the Atlantic. This led to a helpless population of homeless women and children. Britain's solution was to auction them off as well. During the 1650s, over 100,000 Irish children between the ages of 10 and 14 were taken from their parents and sold as slaves in the West Indies, Virginia and New England. In this decade, 52,000 Irish (mostly women and children) were sold to Barbados and Virginia. Another 30,000 Irish men and women were also transported and sold to the highest bidder. In 1656, Cromwell ordered that 2000 Irish children be taken to Jamaica and sold as slaves to English settlers.

Many people today will avoid calling the Irish slaves what they truly were: Slaves. They'll come up with terms like "Indentured Servants" to describe what occurred to the Irish. However, in most cases from the 17th and 18th centuries, Irish slaves were nothing more than human cattle.

As an example, the African slave trade was just beginning during this same period. It is well recorded that African slaves, not tainted with the stain of the hated Catholic theology and more expensive to purchase, were often treated far better than their Irish counterparts.".…., so this is a brief summary of how humans have been discriminated all across the demographics throughout the world since generations."…………….

Racism is a worldwide phenomenon. In some countries it's met with disapproval, in others with denial. People do not want to appear racist or prejudiced, and so many in the West find themselves unable to criticize religious practices, even including those that ought to be criticized. But there are right ways, and wrong ways, to criticize Islam. Racism, xenophobia and anti-Muslim tirades are morally wrong, yet serious discussion of ethnic/religious diversity and its place in society is a long-standing taboo.

There are many more countries in the world which have record of serious racial discrimination, countries like "Australia" where the aboriginals who are the original habitant of Australia, these aboriginals for several hundreds of years have suffered social injustice.

Indian sub-continent has had and have lots of "Racial, Religious and ethnic" related issues, in Indian sub-continent, there are so many ethnic minorities and each of these ethnic group have their own "prejudice" against other, which leads to bitter rivalry, hatred and discriminations.

Racism is a matter of growing concern amongst the nations of the world. Far from being a social ill restricted to one or two countries, the moral disease of racism spans communities, countries, and continents. Racism is a complex issue. At the core of any working definition of racism is the unspoken ingredient of fear. People around the world all belong to the same human "race," they share the same tendencies to fear, domination and subjugation. Hence, inevitably, racism is a world-wide issue. **Darwin's controversial theory of evolution** has contributed to the ignorance fuelling racial conflicts. Over the years people and nations exhibiting higher degrees of civilization have been deemed racially superior.

Chapter 3

Article title **"Racism-Global issue"** stated, "From the institutionalized racism especially in colonial times, when racial beliefs — even eugenics — were not considered something wrong, to recent times where the effects of neo-Nazism is still felt, Europe is a complex area with many cultures in a relatively small area of land that has seen many conflicts throughout history. (Many of these conflicts have had trade, resources and commercial rivalry at their core, but national identities have often added fuel to some of these conflicts).

In its modern form, racism evolved in tandem with European exploration and conquest of much of the rest of the world, and especially after Christopher Columbus reached the Americas. As new peoples were encountered, fought, and ultimately subdued, theories about "race" began to develop, and these helped many to justify the differences in position and treatment of people whom they categorized as belonging to different races.

A possible source of racism is the misunderstanding of Charles Darwin's theories of evolution. Some took Darwin's theories to imply that since some "races" were more civilized, there must be a biological basis for the difference.

At the same time they appealed to biological theories of moral and intellectual traits to justify racial oppression. There is a great deal of controversy about race and intelligence, in part because the concepts of both race and IQ are themselves controversial."----

Although old style racism and the use of racial epithets have gradually diminished in many countries, subtler forms of racism have flourished, is this change an improvement.

Here I would like to discuss about two individual who have been great survivor of "Religious Prejudice and Racism" and both of them have gone on to become phenomenon success story, both are from political field, yes, I'm talking about "Mrs Sonia Gandhi" brave Indian politician and above all "Mr Barak Hussein Obama" the President of United States of America.

Mrs Sonia Gandhi is an Italian born "blonde" woman, who married into an famous Indian Political family of "Nehru/Gandhi," She married former Indian Prime Minister "Rajiv Gandhi" in the 1960s and became Indian citizen, after unfortunate incident when her husband "Rajiv Gandhi" a "former Prime Minister of India" who was tragically assassinated, Sonia Gandhi after spending nearly 7 years in confinement of her house, a widow "Mrs Sonia Gandhi" in the year 1998 decided to take plunge in Indian Politics and she was given the charge of leading her husband's political party and India's biggest ruling Political party the "Indian National Congress," The principle opposition party of India and staunch opponent of Indian National Congress Party, The "Bharatiya Janata Party" a fundamentalist Hindu Right wing party bitterly opposed Mrs Sonia Gandhi being made supreme leader of Indian National Congress.

The Bharatiya Janata Party which believes in hard line Hindutava philosophy, hence it tried making life miserable for Mrs Sonia Gandhi, the members of "Bharatiya Janata Party" passed derogatory racial comments against Mrs Gandhi also attacked her for the religion she belonged too, Mrs Sonia Gandhi took bitter criticism and racial slur by her opponent in her strides and marched ahead, she led her Party the "Indian National Congress" to power and made it the ruling party of India again in the year 2004, Mrs Sonia Gandhi went on to gain international fame and is counted among the most powerful woman in the world.

About "Mr Barak Hussein Obama," when Mr Obama was running for presidency post of the great nation "United States of America," he had an uphill task ahead of him, Mr Barak Obama had to encounter some real torrid moments, from within his own "Democratic Party" as well as the opposite "Republican Party," his opponents from within and from opposition loss no opportunity to remind the voters about "Mr Barak Obama's" "Race and his Religion," Mr Obama son of mixed "Race" and by Religion a half Jew and half Muslim.

Mr Obama's opponents and his detractors did not missed any opportunity in reminding voters of America about Mr Obama's "Race and his Religion" his opponents desperately emphasize on his middle name "Hussein" Mr Obama opponents and rivals emphatically and deliberately emphasising on Mr Obama's middle name "Hussein" to indicate and to make people of America know that Mr Obama has a Muslim connection, well but once all said and done Mr Barak Obama went on to become a great survivor of "racism and religious prejudice," he moved ahead in life gaining from strength to strength.

We must thank god that it was Mr Barak Obama in power and at the helm of affairs in "USA" at the time when rather unexpectedly "Arab Spring" (political crisis and rebellion in Arabian countries) surface in the Arab world, Mr Obama showed great resilience and did not get provoke when there were strong voices heard, many people's group as well as many power centres tried their best to involve America militarily into the "Arab Spring" conflict, Mr Obama circumspect as ever, he respected the people's mandate given to him.

The Americans gave mandate and gave power to Mr Obama by making him president of "USA" only because they knew that this man Mr Obama will restrain from indulging in any kind of war and will ensure that American soldiers do not loose there life fighting battle overseas, because the Americans were fed up with the Republicans, the Americans had in their mind the horrific and excruciating memory of the brave American soldiers who had lost their lives fighting in Pakistan and Afghanistan and Iraq.

So these is how it happens, whosoever we maybe, whether in corridor of power or on high street or on busy crowded street, at times, we just can't escape or prevent ourselves from unfortunate immoral events which at times devastate us and causes mental stress,

Discrimination and social injustice is and has always been so prevalent, let us discuss something more in these regard.

Is it racist to use "White" to describe "Europeans and Americans"?

Is it racist to use the term "Non White" to describe people of colour?

Although many people are quick to detect and condemn instances of racial prejudice, white privileges often goes undetected, what explains this difference?

What is the difference between equal opportunity and affirmative action? Do the two policies contradict each other?

Is it racist for athletic teams to use names such as "Red skin, Indians and Black skin," if it is racist for teams to use such names, than, is it racist to watch their games?

Do we support or oppose the idea of racial profiling (for eg: an Arab subject to greater security check at airports)? If profiling on basis of "Race" is wrong, is it also wrong to profile on the basis of gender? For instance, is it wrong for a woman walking alone to take greater protective measures to encounter male gender than a female stranger?

In case of adoption, should agencies should try and match the "Race" of the children and parents, or should adoption be carried out in a "race" blind manner?

Is it wrong to have an all-Black student dormitory? What about an all-white dormitory? Does the question depends upon minority-majority status?

Does the existence of Black, Latino and Asian student group combat racism, reinforce separatism, both or neither?

One of the least charming but most persistent aspects of human nature is our capacity to hate people who are different. Racism, sexism, ageism, it seems like all the major social categories come with their own "-ism", each fuelled by regrettable prejudice and bigotry.

Emotional trauma and mental health effects from discrimination and stereotyping results in the most significant harm to an individual. There are other damages, such as loss of job or promotional opportunities, loss of pay for days not worked, and damage to reputation.

The people that discriminate or stereotype usually choose scapegoats on whom to take out their frustration and aggression. They choose those who are seen as weaker or inferior to themselves.

It is very important to know that parents that practice discrimination can pass it on to their children in a number of ways. In fact, children learn to discriminate in the same way they absorb a new language, learn to dress in a certain way, or to use a toy. Early child and family experiences shape peoples' attitudes and behaviours.

Harm from racial discrimination results from both first-hand and personal experiences; witnessing racism is as stressful as being subjected to it.

Article title **"Stereotyping Has Lasting Negative Impact"** finding of their studies found; "Aggression. Over-eating. Inability to focus. Difficulty making rational decisions. New research out of the University of Toronto Scarborough shows prejudice has a lasting negative impact on those who experience it.

"Past studies have shown that people perform poorly in situations where they feel they are being stereotyped," said Professor Michael Inzlicht of psychology, who led the study, published edition of the *Journal of Personality and Social Psychology*. "What we wanted to do was look at what happens afterwards. Are there lingering effects of prejudice? Does being stereotyped have an impact beyond the moment when stereotyping happens?"

In order to determine whether negative stereotyping in a particular situation had lasting effects, Inzlicht's team performed a series of tests. First, they placed participants in situations where they had to perform a task in the face of negative stereotyping. After the participants were removed from the prejudicial situation, researchers measured their ability to control their aggression, eat appropriate amounts, make rational decisions, and stay focused.

Their results show that prejudice and stereotyping have lingering adverse impacts.

"Even after a person leaves a situation where they faced negative stereotypes, the effects of coping with that situation remain," says Inzlicht. "People are more likely to be aggressive after they've faced prejudice in a given situation. They are more likely to exhibit a lack of self-control. They have trouble making good, rational decisions. And they are more likely to over-indulge on unhealthy foods."

In one portion of the study, researchers had a group of women write a mathematic test. They told the women this test would determine whether or not they were capable and smart in math's, subtly injecting stereotypes about women's and mathematic skills "into the air," said Inzlicht. A separate group of women wrote the same test, except this group was given support and coping strategies to deal with the stress they'd face when writing the test.

After completing the mathematic test, the two groups performed another series of tasks designed to gauge their aggression levels, their ability to focus and to exercise self-control.

"In these follow-up tests, the women who felt discriminated against ate more than their peers in the control group. They showed more hostility than the control group. And they performed more poorly on tests that measured their cognitive skills," said Inzlicht.

The pattern remained the same, regardless of the test groups. People who felt they were discriminated against - whether based on gender, age, race or religion - all experienced significant impacts even after they were removed from the situation, says Inzlicht.

"These lingering effects hurt people in a very real way, leaving them at a disadvantage," said Inzlicht. "Even many steps removed from a prejudicial situation, people are carrying around this baggage that negatively impacts their lives."……..

The victims of discrimination exhibit a wide range of responses as discussed, from emotional devastation to physical illness and other symptoms, to militancy and protest, to the exaggeration or complete denial of the whole experience.

Not applying diversity may result in economic costs, such as lower local revenues due to decreased local expenditures by residents, etc. So if you don't want your work-place to be a hostile environment or even become the next murder scene, practice diversity, and train your managers and employees to eliminate discrimination, prejudice and stereotype.

Racial discrimination is carried out individually or structurally with equally adverse consequences. When perpetuated structurally and institutionally, racism can diminish a group's collective capacity to promote the advancement and progress of its members.

If we take the effects of racism against the African American population as an example, it has been noticed that racism can lead to an unexplained prevalence of hypertension among them. It has also been alleged that there is a link between the prevalence of hypertension and racial discrimination at work and with the media portraying racism and continuous racial discrimination.

The persons holding constitution post needs to be more bolder and pragmatic and should provide strong leadership, for example; there are countries that host events be it political or cultural or sporting events, when the countries are inviting people from other countries to visit there country to attend any events, these governments should first ensure that their own folks behave well with the visiting guest or tourist who visit there country.

There are instances when we people travel to countries whether on official visit or otherwise, for example: to be spectators to watch sporting events or cultural shows, the host nation citizens at times behave rudely they are offensive in their behaviour and attitude and intolerant towards the "Race or Religion" of us, they taunt us and make derogatory caustic comments which devastate us, here I would like to refer to one brazen behaviour issue, when in 1936 the Olympics were being held in Germany, the "Nazi' Press" use to call the black American athletes "black auxiliaries" and the Racist prejudice "German government" had even requested the withdrawal of blacks "African American" from participation in the Olympic event, so, this is what happens, if the persons holding the top constitutional post are themselves not sincere in their effort and not committed and disciplined, hence, one cannot expect its citizens to be tolerant and respect people of different "Races and Religions."

There are many governments, and as usual as they are supposed to do, that is, these countries governments "Tourism department" as part of their effort to promote their country as a destination for international "Tourism" and to lure citizens from other country to visit there country, such countries government tourism department and tourism ministry will launch major "Tourism Promotional Advertisement Campaign" all over the world, these governments tourism department spends huge amount of money and goes out of their way to woo and to attract people from other nations to visit their nation to spend leisure time and holidays in their country, most countries tourism departments compete among each other, and ensure that their advertisement gets maximum mileage, they try to woo people from other country by showing the best images of their country photographs highlighting scenic beauty and landscape of their country and also they emphasis on the fact that their country's hospitality is among the best and every person who visit their country will thoroughly enjoy the hospitality of their country.

Now when we people actually fall prey to such promotional advertisement of any particular country and when we visit any these country, more often we do enjoy, but "NO" there are many unfortunate people for whom travelling to a particular country becomes a nightmare, there are many countries where contrary to the expectation of great hospitality, many a time when we are traveling to a country as tourist or otherwise, their happens to be many perverts in that society who often misbehave with tourist or guest of their country, these perverts are either verbally offensive to us or they try to take undue advantage they cheat or mug us, there are instances when tourist are robbed in restaurant not long before they arrive in the city, visiting tourist are stripped of thousands of Dollars and some callous do not hesitate in flicking away with the passports of tourists.

Leave alone to under-develop countries but even the most advance and developed nations too have comprehensively failed in protecting the interest of tourist and in providing adequate safety and security to the foreign nationals and the visitors to their nation.

So the onus of safety lies on the leadership of the country, the leadership needs to take ownership and the constitutional head of the country needs to first educate their own citizens first to be more cordial and accommodative and more hospitable towards the visiting guest or tourist in their country.

Many times its notice that the shopkeepers and Taxi's drivers and others are very hostile and arrogant with the tourist who has come to their country to spend his/her holidays.

After all it's not the beauty of your house that will impress the guest who has come to your home, it's your hospitality that'll live a lasting impression on your guest about you.

It's a recurring nightmare for racism related discrimination in sports, again the host nation that is hosting sporting events in their country are more often frivolous, many a time the sporting personalities become victim of "Racism" these instances are very common when sports players have to listen abusive and sleazy comments from the ruthless spectators sitting in the stadium stands or at times when these sports players are often roughed up in "Hotels or Bars and Restaurants," people should realize that these sporting players or artists are performing for the pride of the country they represents and to entertain the larger audience, high profile sporting personalities and movie stars are considered to be goodwill cultural ambassadors.

Like sports and cultural shows or like fashion and glamour, even in "education institutions" with the students as well it's the same recurring nightmare of "Religious Prejudice and Racism," particularly so these discrimination happens in the most developed countries of the world even in countries which have been rated as the most peaceful country in the world, their citizens are intolerant towards people who come to study in their country, the citizens of most developed nations as well are xenophobic.

Again like the countries that promote tourism, there are many country that promotes educational tourism, specially they come to countries such as "India, China and other Asian countries as well as they go to Africa" to attract youngster to visit their country and to enrol themselves in universities, for higher studies and to do degree course, The develop nations put up large Advertisements on social media as well as print media, they promise the youngster from Asia and Africa as in how good the qualification of the university in their country is, and they also assures the youths that how much beneficial it will be for them with regards to their future and career prospects for learning and passing degree course from the university of their country.

Every youngsters "boys and girls" are always craving for excellent academic and career opportunity, most youths particularly from India takes educational loans and fulfils their dream of pursuing higher academic education, with lots of dreams in their eyes many youngster from Asia and Africa travel to develop nations like "Australia, United States, Canada or New Zealand etc," now, once these students lands in any of these country, for some maybe things fall in place and they settle down well, but, few of them and these few are lots in number, for few less-fortunate individuals at times their dream turns into nightmare.

There have been countless such instances and incident when the youngsters who go to develop countries for higher studies for lucrative degree course, there have been reports of many students youngsters have been harassed and humiliated on the streets or in universities campus as well as there are many instances when many of them have been killed, so, again whose responsibility is it, why do the political leadership of the country fail to protect the innocent? after all these youngsters come to your country for higher studies not purely because of their own choice or maybe their own choice that they came for studies but isn't it also a fact that your country's universities also promote itself and woos the youngsters from other countries particularly from the under-develop or developing nations.

Indians bemoan a lot that they are much more prone to racial discrimination when they go abroad for higher studies or for technical training or for job.

Let's see, how good Indians are and how tolerant they are in their own country? Interesting to know that India is a big highly populated country in the world with diverse culture and many ethnic communities.

When citizens from "North-Eastern" part of India, visits the mainland India in search of job or for higher education, these "North-Eastern" Indians again not all but many of them feel like "pariah" in their own country, yes, many Indians display indifferent attitude towards their "North-East" compatriots, because these people from "North-East' India" are racially different from the mainland Indians, they look more like Chinese, hence some miscreant from mainland India address them as "Chinky" which many from "North-East' Indians" feel is offensive language, but apart from that as well these folks from "North-East' India" have to suffer in many other ways, it is difficult for them to get accommodation as many Indians from mainland India have some "Prejudice" about the character of these North-East' Indians."

Also there are many other "Race and Religion" related issues and discrimination, as India is largely a Hindu majority country, and this "Hindu" religion is divided into many different caste and community, but the biggest divide in Hinduism is the "Upper caste and the Lower caste," hence one always gets to see socio-cultural divide among the Hindu's, more often the Hindu's belonging to the so-called "upper caste" discriminate against the Hindu's of "lower caste," in most Indian schools and universities as well as in many work places one gets to witness bitter Tiff between the so-called "upper caste and lower caste" Hindu's, at times the trouble gets further confounded when the folks from Muslim community as well intervene between warring "Hindu" factions, just to remind that Muslim religion is a big minority religion in India.

The skills and talents of members of minorities in our societies, whether they are citizens of the countries in which they live or more recent migrants, needs to be acknowledged, and furthermore to be better utilised. A proactive approach that appreciates diversity while furthering integration would help to reduce racial discrimination and increase security, as well as helping to boost growth.

There is a difference between "Reacting and Responding," when you "React" you allow your external circumstances to call shots, when you "Respond" your action and feeling distinguish distinction.

So, what happens is, That, while we are reacting to things or events, we often are not in control of our thoughts, for example: when we see it or are shown "video or photographic images" of events or incidents of brutality or callousness, we often get outrageous and our reactions are swift and severe, we are quick to either sympathize or we get fierce and furious.

The Politicians or Religious leaders or some Individuals with vested interest often exploit the most vulnerable individuals or group of peoples by showing them images of violence and crime or hatred to ignite their passion, thereby "these unscrupulous elements" subtly encourage the most vulnerable section of society to turn hostile and support them in their nefarious plan, this is how people from a particular section of society are "Radicalize," divisions are cause among civil society, populations gets bitterly "Polarize" on "Religious or Racist" line.

There also exist vast number of people within our civil society, these are the kind people, who generally are very circumspect, who don't allow their "emotions to run high" instead these lot of people have tendency to go into the reasons of things before they decide or plan their "move" and they do not react to the prevailing situation in haste, but instead "response" very cautiously, they don't get easily provoke "whenever any kind or type of provocative images or materials are flaunted in front of them or any kind of stories about any incidents are narrated to them.

So, it always is in our interest, that, not to let our emotions run high, always find reason to go into reasons and only than either "React or Response" to matter or issues concerning us or to the civil society at large.

Many would like to know as in, why are "Arab or Muslims" subject to greater security checks at airports or otherwise?

There has been a long history of religious prejudice. For example, Christianity is guilty of terrible crimes against Judaism over the last 2,000 years. Every Jew in England was expelled, and the last few were chased into a tower that was set alight - they burned to death. However, when Hitler murdered 6 million Jews, it was race, not faith, that was the criteria.

Around the world there are many complex situations where religion can further complicate things. Sometimes religion is a major cause of problems, other times it's just another factor, or may even be used as an excuse. Often, ignorance just worsens a difficult situation. The press doesn't always help, reinforcing stereotypes and publicising only negative stories. For example, many people are currently very concerned about Islamophobia- Muslims are hated or distrusted, and used as scapegoats

Yes, why? The Muslims, it's a fact but a very disturbing fact, as in, why should Muslims be subject to more intense and thorough check? Why are everyone and everywhere in the world, the "security authorities" are suspicious of a person belonging to a Muslim community?

Let's find out, as to, what is it that makes people belonging to other religions and communities more insecure with regards to Muslims?

More importantly, why in this world every Non-Islamic "Religious community" no matter how so ever bitter rivals they maybe or no matter whatsoever differences these religious communities may have between them? But, there is only one thing which unites every "Non-Islamic religious community" and that is their "resolve" to oppose "Islam," yes, every "Non-Islamic' religion" consider "Islam" their bitter "foe" hence when it comes to dealing with Islam all these "Non-Islamic' religion" will sink their differences and unite to take on Islam. But, why?

Islamophobia existed in premise before the terrorist attacks of September 11, 2001 in "US," but it increased in frequency and notoriety during the past decade. An exaggerated fear, hatred, and hostility toward Islam and Muslims that is perpetuated by negative stereotypes resulting in bias, discrimination, and the marginalization and exclusion of Muslims from social, political, and civic life.

Since September 11.2001, there have been reports on increases in racial profiling, at airports, particularly targeting people who appear to be Muslim or of South Asian or middle eastern descent, It has been a routine practice by law enforcement officials to stop individuals who are profiled because of their race and religious and ethnic appearance or who may appear to be "suspicious

Yes, very true, after the terror incident that happened in United States of America on "11th sept 2001," the religious prejudice with regards to Muslim religion, that, all or most "Muslims" are considered pro-terrorist, however is these perception that many folks of different Non-Islamic religions have about Members of Muslim community, are such people right in their belief? No, maybe not, Islam as religion has diverse philosophy and ideology, not every Islamist ideology teaches and practise violence.

Every Muslims are not terrorist is true but every Muslims also do not strongly and vehemently oppose the terrorist, Now, Yes, this is the reason and this is an answer.

Many Muslims observe their religion and live their lives with no intent to either support or oppose fundamentalist extremism. Some critics proclaim that because mainstream Muslims fail to act against extremists, it allows extremists to prosper. Because Muslims even those faction of Islam that otherwise do not believe in violence and have never involved themselves with any kind of terror activity or ever supported extremist Islamist Jihadist elements, None of the Muslim factions has ever come out in open and vehemently oppose or disassociated themselves from the monstrous elements within Islam, which teaches its followers and preaches and practise abrasive Islamic "Sharia Law" which believes and justifies in killing "Non-Muslims."

The ruthless Islamic "Sunni" extremist terrorist group such as "Al-Shabaab, Boko-Haram, Al-Qaeda and ISIS (Islamic state of Iraq and Syria), these callous terrorist group having set-up their terror camp and bases in African and Arabian peninsula countries, have terrorise the whole region, these terrorist group brazenly kidnap and rape women, desecrate and burn places of worship, kill and slaughter people, bully and intimidate people of minority religious communities like Shia Muslims, Kurdish, Jewish and Christians. The Sunni Muslims disregard and disrespect every other religion and calls them apostate and infidels, as if every other "non-Sunni Muslim" religious communities are evil and have no right to leave on this planet earth.

Islamic Terrorism has severely impacted the economy and has harm the livelihood of millions, the thriving tourism industry in countries like Kenya and Egypt have been devastated because of sporadic terror attack in these countries, thereby rendering millions job less.

Because the various faction of Islam (Particularly the Islamic factions who have impeccable track records of peace and harmony in civil society) have not been able to convince the Non-Islamic community of the world, that they honestly and sincerely oppose such elements who are extremist radicals and those who are killing and harming the innocents people, they have never severely condemn the terrorist elements, instead to make matters worse, most people from Islamic community always "dilly-dally" in condemning the Islamic terrorist activity, and to make matters even worse many members from Muslim community finds vague reasons and purpose to speak in favour of terrorist, thereby sending wrong signals and setting wrong impression in the minds of "Non-Islamic communities," that's, what has precipitated crisis for Muslim community, and these is what, perhaps maybe the reason, as in, why the members of Muslim communities are more often suspected and are often subject to intense security checks.

Message, to Muslim "brothers and sisters," till the time you "Muslim" folks will dilly-dally, and have double standards like hypocrites and until such time y'all will not convince the outside world and the global communities, that you all are genuine in your resolve in fighting against the jihadist and are honestly oppose to any kind of terrorist activity, till such time, the Non-Islamic community of the world will find it hard to trust y'all, and also to note another fact is, that not just Non-Islamic countries where the members of Muslim community is subject to more thorough and intense security check, but, quite ironically, even in Muslim rule countries the members of Muslim community are looked upon with suspicion and are thoroughly checked even at airports of countries which are ruled by Muslims.

Chapter 4

We live in the world full of different prejudices. Millions of people are discriminated by racial, cultural, religious, gender and lots of other prejudices. It seems that various kinds of prejudice have always existed. Just in the course of history they change a bit or emerges in some new forms.

Prejudice is a negative social phenomenon, which can be easily described. This is, in fact, Think about common social problems that are related to prejudices, tell whether it is possible to eliminate such problems from our society.

The elimination of prejudice movement creates long lasting community change by addressing the underlying differences between people that prevent progress.

Religious prejudice, yes, Religious Prejudice, is the worse type of Prejudice.

What role does religion plays in our life?

Do we need religions to exist? If so, why?

Has religion done anything worthwhile or good for humans? Or, various religious beliefs that exist in this world, has simply harmed humans more than it has helped?

Does religion unites humans or creates wedge and divides humans?

Many contentious and burning questions with regards to "Religions," but, do we have answers, for it? And if we have answers to the burning questions with regards to religions, ok, but, do we have any solutions? Yes, of course, there are solutions, but, are we humans resolutely in favour of implementing those solutions.

Let's discuss the matter further, let us find out how effective or ineffective religion is.

Religion does three things quite effectively, Divides People, Controls People, Deludes People.

Karl Marx saw religion as a political tool utilized by the oppressing ruling classes, arguing that it is in the interest of the ruling classes to instil in the masses the religious conviction that their current suffering will lead to eventual happiness, so that they will not attempt to make any genuine effort to understand and overcome the real source of their sufferings. It was on this basis that he described religion as "the opium of the people."

Yes, religions have played destructive role rather than constructive role, various different religions have only caused divisions among humans and have done little to unite humans.

"Birds of a feather flocks together;" this proverb means, people like and prefer to stay with people of their own community, they feel discomfort and like "pariah" when they are not among people of their own community.

I have seen and observed as well as felt it, and it pains, I have seen "Mothers" advising and ordering their children as to whom they should talk too and whom they should avoid talking too, many if not all "parents" want their children to mingle with and socialize with children's of their own community or children's of equal socio-strata.

Overtly or Subtly; Nepotism and favouritism exist everywhere, many influential figures in the civil society, likes to promote person of their own community, and these same influential figures at time may not hesitate in systematically sabotaging the fortune of a person "despite" the fact that he/she may have right merit and credentials for the available "opportunity.

Many family own business in particular will always prefer and hire "employees" belonging to their own Religion, whenever there will be need of professionals service of any kind or purpose, they will often hire professional who hails from their own "Religion."

There are "power brokers" who have their own vested interest and sly motives, and these discreet power centres have for Thousands of years used religion as a vital tool to Radicalize people and polarize the civil society on "Ethnic and Religious' line," this is a very vicious circle, Peoples patience runs out, when they are provoked and instigated in the name of religion, These Radical minded people then can go to any extent in harming others, Their emotions and thoughts are with the religion they belong too, they do not bother and shows no remorse for the peoples who do not belong to their religion.

So much talk about religions, now let us at least find out some startling facts about few of the most prominent religions, to make a note of things as to how true and genuine are the teachings and attributes of these prominent religions as every religions should be open for scrutiny.

Most people's emotions are deeply attached to their religion and religious belief, most of us, like to scrutinize and like to find fault in other religions, but when someone talks or reminds us about the fault and highlights negative aspect in our religion then many among us "people" reacts fiercely and furiously, that's, what it is, its bitter but its truth, people like to look at the fault in others but when talk to them about their fault and shortcomings in them, these people ignore it and looks the other way, such a hypocrites are these people.

Call "spade a spade" call "niggard a niggard," "like it or not" the truth needs to be spoken.

Among the most influential and powerful religions, to name a few are, Islam "the most powerful religion," Christianity "the most dominant religion," Hinduism and Buddhism "are very philosophical religions," and "Judaism" not a very large religion but members of this religion are arguably the most intellectual and talented people of the whole lot.

Let's start discussion by first knowing about Islam.

Islam is the religion which was founded sometime in the "7th century" by a man known as "Mohammed" who belonged to Qureshi tribe (pagan), Prophet Mohammed as he's known, and he's been branded by his followers as "Allah's Apostle" and he's been given a title "messenger of peace."

On the positive side, the followers of Islam are extremely helpful and generous, the people of Muslim community are always ready to render their help and support to others.

What are Islamic "sharia law"? Sharia Laws are the guideline and rules set for every person of Islam to follow it, most of the Sharia laws were or are rulings of Prophet Mohammed himself, but periodically some of these Sharia law have been amended by various different faction of Islam.

How peace loving and disciplined are these "Sharia Laws," and Prophet Mohammed "the' messenger of peace."

Islam is totalitarian ideology that rejects Democracy, Personal freedom and every other religions, Hatred is Preached as Divine Prophecy against all thing not Muslim.

Islam is anything but peaceful, Allah's dearest Apostle "Prophet Mohammed's" few "Key" features and prominent ruling of Sharia law.

Forbidden by Sharia, such as Adultery or eating forbidden foods or drinking alcoholic beverages, but most heinous and draconian part of Sharia Laws are like, Stoning to Death a woman who's found of committing Adultery, and also the "Gays and Lesbians" are to be severely punished by stoning to death, and chop off the hands of a person who's proved guilty of stealing or robbing.

Calling the Non-Islamic people "Infidels" and as per "Sharia" it is "Ok" for every practising Muslims to harm the interest off or do not hesitate even a bit to even kill the infidels, as per the Islamic belief all Non-Muslims are "Infidels" because they consider these infidels to be the enemy of god and enemy of the Allah's Apostle (Prophet Mohammed) hence its Ok to kill or harm the infidels, show no remorse or mercy for these infidels.

Also, as per "Sharia law," severely punish or even kill the "Apostate," The Prophet said, if somebody "a Muslim" discards his religion, kill him/her, for example: a man who embrace Islam then reverts back to his Previous religion, is to be killed according to the verdict of Allah's Apostle.

Allah's Apostle "Prophet Mohammed's" though branded as "messenger of peace," but this peaceful person in his life time also lead and fought as many as

"Seventeen" battles, each of his war and battles resulted in deaths of "who knows" how many? But obviously thousands and thousands may have died.

To mention few of the "Key" battles "Allah's Apostle" Prophet Mohammed fought.

Under the leadership of Prophet Mohammed, his army brutally attacked the Jewish Tribe of "Qurayza," in this battle Prophet Mohammed's army killed nearly 700 hundred Jews.

The infamous battle of "Khaybar," The Allah's Apostle "Prophet Mohammed" won the battle of Khaybar and his army was ordered to behead all the Jews.

The warriors of "Prophet Mohammed" conquered "Mecca" and established the first religious Dictatorship in the world, banning all other "Gods."

Islam and its founder the so-called "Allah's Apostle" are nothing but "Two head snake."

Now, let find out few things about other most dominant religion in the world, The Christianity.

As per noted "Scholars and Historians," there's no credible evidence which proves, that **"Jesus of Nazareth"** ever existed in flesh or blood, He is simply of Mythical or Fictional character created by the early Christian community.

Jesus is Mythicism or simply "Mythicism" is the proposition that Jesus of Nazareth never existed, even if he "did" he had virtually nothing to do with the founding of Christianity, there are no Non-Christian to Jesus Christ from the first century, and that Christianity has strong "Pagan and Mythical" roots.

So, Jesus was neither historical nor divine.

Now, how did Christianity came into effect, and, who is the real inventor of this religion Christianity? Let's find out.

Christianity is a copycat religion created by Roman Emperor "Constantine" for political purpose, based upon a myth.

The Persian saviour God "Mithra" was crucified in 600B.C? or 400 B.C? Which was based on other similar myth, all the way back to Chrishna of India (a mythical God that some claim was "crucified" around 1200 B.C).

There were 16 mythical "Crucifixion" before Christ, The belief is the Crucifixion of Gods was prevalent in various oriental or heathen countries, long prior to the reported Crucifixion of Christ.

Of the 16 Crucifixion most were born of a virgin and about half of them on December 25th.

Christianity was invented by the Great Roman Emperor Constantine for political purpose in 325 AD, based on the myth of Mithra (Persian saviour god born on 25th December).

There were too many religions in Rome, in 325 A.D a council was called in an endeavour to amalgamate the many religions of Roman Empire into one.

Christianity plagiarized older myths and legends historicized to suit the Roman catholic church, while combining the numerous religions existing at the time (Krishna, Horus, Mithraism, Osirian, Isis and many other mystery religions), for unity and to stop all conflict between the numerous religions.

Eusebius (Bishop of Caesarea in Palestine "father of church) Eusebius who was Constantine friend, hence, he helped Emperor Constantine establish Christianity.

Let us find out the truth of two of the Christians principle festivals "Christmas and Easter."

Christians have been conditioned to accept that Christmas and Easter are essentially part of the Christian tradition. The fact is neither is at all Christian and both have their roots in the mystery cults, The Saturnalia, the worship of the mother-goddess system and the worship of the sun god, they are directly contradictory to the laws of God and his system.

The Saturnalia: there was a festival celebrated in December in Rome. It is necessary to any understanding of, what is happening at Christmas? That festival was termed the Saturnalia, it was a festival of Saturn to whom the inhabitant of Latium, the Latin's attributed agriculture and the arts necessary for civilised life, it fell towards the end of December and was viewed by the population as a time of absolute relaxation and merriment.

During its continuance, the law courts were closed, No Public business could be transacted. The school kept holiday, slaves were relieved of onerous toils and permitted to wear the Pileus or badge of freedom, they were granted freedom of speech and were waited on at special banquet by their Masters whose clothes they wore (Ibid) all rank devoted themselves to feasting and Mirth with present exchange among friends.

And about "Easter,"

The name "Easter" comes from occult and pagan celebration of their spring goddess "Eostre and Ishtar," The Babylonians and other Pagan cultures had a spring festival in honour of their goddess of spring and rebirth. **Easter Friday** is also a pagan celebration timed to be on the third full "Moon Day" from the start of the year.

So this is how Christianity was invented (basically for political purpose), hence of both the two major religion "Islam and Christianity" while there is nothing peaceful about Islam religion and the Christianity is nothing but a "Sham."

Like the Christians festivals of "Christmas and Easter," the Islamic traditional rituals like performing "Haj and Fasting in the month of Ramadan" are also copied from the age old pagan rituals. The pagan borrowings constitute significant facets of Islam and Christianity.

The difference between pre-Islamic Ramadan and Islamic Ramadan, is, pre-Islamic Ramadan was practiced by a Pagan tribe in Arabia, and Islamic Ramadan is practiced by Muslims all over the world. During Ramadan, Pagan Arabs used to abstain from food, water, sexual contact etc. Muslims practice the same Pagan Ramadan rituals.

Ramadan, the ninth month of the Islamic calendar and the rigid observance of thirty days of fasting during the daylight hours, has Pagan roots developed in India and the Middle-East. The observance of fasting to honour the moon, and ending the fast when the moon's crescent appears, was practised with the rituals of the Eastern worshippers of the moon. Both Ibn al-Nadim and the Shahrastani tells us about al-Jandrikinieh, an Indian sect which began to fast when the moon disappeared and ended the fast with a great feast when the crescent reappeared.

It is a well-known fact that Islam adapted the Pagan practice of fasting. There is a Hadith in Sahih Bukhari that mentions the ritual. '*Ashura* was a day on which the tribe of Quraish used to fast in the pre-Islamic period of ignorance. The Prophet also used to fast on this day. So when he migrated to Medina, he fasted on it and ordered (the Muslims) to fast on it. When the fasting of Ramadan was enjoined, it became optional for the people to fast or not to fast on the day of Ashura.' The fasting for *Ashura* (10th of Muharram) originated from a Quraish Pagan practice. Ramadan fasting came later from Sabian tradition. Sabians are mentioned in several verses of the Quran along with Christians and Jewish. Sabians, a non-Muslim Iraqi tribe, believed in monotheism, observed fasting 30 days a year, and prayed 5 times a day.

The Sabians, who were pagans in the Middle-East, were identified in two groups, the Mandaeans and the Harranians. The Mandaeans lived in Iraq during the 2nd century A.D. as they continue to do today, they worshipped multiple gods, or "light personalities." The other group, considered as Sabians were the Harranians. They worshipped Sin, the moon, as their main deity, but they also worshipped planets and other deities.

Nabeel Afsar "under Enlightenment, Islam" comments: "there's more. It turns out that the pagans also prayed five times a day facing towards the Kaaba. And before they prayed, they performed ritual washing or ablution. And most curiously, the pagans also had a common saying that was the central tenet of many of their faiths: "There is no god but God." For the unfamiliar, the first pillar of Islam is identical to this mantra with one slight revision: "There is no god but God; and Mohammad is his last messenger." And of course, it's well known that Muslims are required to pray five times daily after performing ritual washing.

So if the ritual of Ramadan was originally conceived to honour the deity of the Moon, why were these practices not destroyed like the idols in the Kaaba? Just like Constantine combined Roman paganism with Christianity to ensure peace & secure power, so too has Islam cannibalized its pagan predecessors to woo converts. Modern Muslims are completely oblivious to the fact that they are actually celebrating the death and rebirth of the Moon deity in accordance with ancient pagan astrology."....

Not only Ramadan fasting, but other Pagan rituals were also Islamized. The Kaaba in Mecca was a centre of idol-worship. 360 idols were kept in the Kaaba. According to Hadith Bukhari 3:43:658 Narrated by "Abdullah bin Masud:" The Prophet entered Mecca and (at that time) there were three hundred-and-sixty idols around the Kaaba. He started stabbing the idols with a stick he had in his hand and reciting: "Truth (Islam) has come and Falsehood (disbelief) has vanished."

The Black-stone or al-Ḥajar al-Aswad of the Kaaba became the central shrine object in Islam. It was one of the many stones and idols venerated by pre-Islamic Pagans. The Black Stone was kissed by people during pre-Islamic pagan worship. Muhammad did not completely abolish Idol worship, he made the Black Stone stay and allowed people to continue the practice of kissing the stone. It is the same pre-Islamic Pagan stone that Muslims kiss today during Hajj and Umrah. The Islamic historians believe that the black stone was a pagan deity called 'Al-Lat', one of the three daughters of Allah, the Pagan moon-god. She was once venerated as a cubic rock at Ta'if in Arabia.

The Kaaba's shape is somewhat cubical. Of note in the Kaaba's structure is a black rock built into the wall in its eastern corner. The black rock's diameter is about 12 inches. It is reddish black in colour, and has red and yellow particles. The black rock is kissed during the perambulation, (the circulation of the Muslims around the Kaaba). The Kaaba is about 50 feet high, and the walls are about 40 feet long. The facade contains the door, which starts at 7 feet off the ground, and faces North-East. To enter the Kaaba, a ladder must be used. Also built in the eastern corner, is another stone called "lucky". This stone is only touched, not kissed.

There were 360 idols around the Kaaba. The pilgrimages to the Kaaba were all pagan pilgrimages, the ritual processions around the Kaaba were part of pagan beliefs and custom, the white robes worn by the pilgrims were from pagan faiths, the veneration of the Kaaba and black stone are derived from pagan rituals and beliefs. Pagans called out the names of their pagan gods as they circled the Kaaba, today, Muslims call out Allah's name. Pagans ran between the nearby hills, Muhammad authorized Muslims to do that in the Quran, and probably ran between the hills himself.

Judaism; is the most beleaguered religion, always it has found itself at the receiving end, both major "Monotheism Religions" Islam and Christianity, even though both "Islam and Christianity" they were born out of and have adopted most of Jewish gods teachings and preaching, yet both Islam but even more severely critical and hostile has been Christianity towards the Jews, The Jewish community always bemoan and disparage the Islamic religion for harming them and their interest, but the fact is that they have been more severely been harmed by the Christians in almost every part of the world, for hundreds of years, the European warlords most of whom belonging to Christian faith have for centuries persecuted the Jews.

Jews in Europe were subjected to progressively harsh persecution that ultimately led to the murder of 6,000,000 Jews. Jews were the victims of Germany's deliberate and systematic attempt to annihilate the entire Jewish population of Europe, the Holocaust known as the Final Solution, which called for the systematic extermination of all Jews and the other scapegoats. It's has been the objective of the Christians to expunge the "Jews" from the world and not the principle objective of Islam.

To talk about other two major religious beliefs "Hinduism and Buddhism" both between them have global population of over Two and Half Billion people.

Buddhism and Hinduism are two side of the same coin, there isn't much socio-cultural difference between these two religions, Buddhism is born out of Hinduism, like "Islam," Buddhism is also branded as religion of peace, but if one looks deep inside the history of the countries where Buddhism is the principle religion, likewise Islam, the history of the countries with majority Buddhist population is nothing but full of agony and violence, crime and hatred, yes, but, one fact is also that many Islamic and well as Buddhist countries are phenomenon economic success and prosperity.

The history of Hinduism is intrinsically linked to that of history of India, Hinduism and Buddhism is more a way of life then a Religions.

The original habitants of India were of dark brown skin "Dravidian' Race, some four thousand or so years ago the Indo-European people supposedly from Russia and Central Asian countries crossed inside the Indian territory by crossing the Indus River valley, The Indo-European Race People as they were called "The Aryans," when the Aryans invaded India, they forcefully pushed the original habitants of India of the Dravidian Race right from the extreme northern parts of India into the interiors of India and more towards the southern parts of India.

The arrival of the Indo-European Aryan "Race" inside Indian Territory, created a bi-polar division in the Indian society.

Dravidians were actually peace loving farmers and they were not trained in any kind of warfare. It is believed that when the Aryans invaded India, they pushed the Dravidians to the Southern part, as the Aryans were skilled fighters and came prepared with weapons and chariots. Also Dravidians, had a very sophisticated culture and used to worship all forms of life like herbs, and plants.

What happen is? That after the arrival of the Aryan "Race," brought in lots of socio-cultural, linguistic and religious changes in the Indian society, which eventually led to conflict in India among "Races" and gradually caste system formation started to happen, this caste system in India became curse for the Indians and has continued to remain so ever since.

Bi-polar division in India between different "Races" and communities, The many caste formation among Hindus led to further division, The two main groups were formed "The Upper Caste Hindus and Lower Caste Hindus" (the so-called lower caste Hindus are considered "untouchable"), The upper caste Hindus consider Lower Caste Hindus of inferior race (the lowest caste in Hindu's are called "Sudras," which happens to mean dark skin in Sanskrit).

Primarily Hindu Society is divided into four Varnas and many castes and sub-castes and thus totally stands not only segmented but fragmented vehemently based on the idea of high and low, superior and inferior, pure and impure, touchable and untouchable.

The Shudras are socially as well as religiously neglected and are not treated as human-beings but are treated even worse than dogs and cats.

For thousands of years the Upper Caste Hindus have carried out atrocities on Lower caste Hindus, heinous crimes of hatred and public humiliation against lower caste Hindus have been prevalent for thousands of years in India, so much public injustice against these so-called lower caste Hindus is that the upper caste Hindus won't let these so-called lower caste Hindus sit next to them and won't drink water or won't allow them to drink water from the same well, the lower caste Hindus are discriminated and are victims of social injustice. Again like Jews, the Hindus as well are critical of Islam, but the Hindus have failed to do introspection of themselves, the Hindus for all their ills blames the Muslims, but these Hindus never look within themselves and do not construe the fact that how aggressively they fight among themselves and how bitterly they are divided among themselves.

The Hindus and the Jews have strong prejudice against Islam, both these religious communities strongly and critically believes that Islam is a monster an evil which has profoundly been harming them. Well both these religions "Hindus and Jews" are not wrong in their senses, yes it's true that in medieval era as well in the contemporary era the Islamic extremism has cause extreme harm and considerable damage both psychologically and physically to both the Hindus and Jews. But once you take a deeper look in history as well in the present times, it is not Islam, but the fact proves that, the Christianity has clobbered both these ancient religions, the Hinduism must not forget the fact the European crusaders having invaded the large Hindu dominated country of "India" and ransacked it carried out atrocities and killing and made Hindus slave in their own country, and for the Jews should not ignored the fact that they've been persecuted and humiliated till date more vigorously in Christian dominated countries, it was in Europe that the Jews were thrown into the gas chambers.

So, the findings is that all the prominent and formidable religions, the fact is that these religions have nothing but hatred and bitterness among them and between them. But the biggest dichotomy is that all three prominent Abrahamic and monotheism religions "Islam, Christians and Jewish" people have for generation after generations been living in illusion, folks of these three religions are basically oblivious of the truth and roots of their religion (particularly, Islam and Christians). Members of these three Abrahamic religious communities never bother to establish the fact with regards to their religion. The minds of believers and followers of "Islam, Christianity and Jews" have for generations been indoctrinated with superstitions and have been strongly embedded in the minds of their followers the divine fear and hatred for their rival community and false belief. And as people of these various religions have so heavily invested their precious time of their life in religious belief and thinking about divine power and reading un-substantive so-called religious holy books, that these people have little time to think about nefarious activity happening around, hence this is and has been the reason why corruption has thrive and how the corrupt and pervert religious politicians and political politicians thrive for past centuries and perhaps will continue to do so for many more hundreds of years.

The facts show a clarity that human kind cannot live in harmony due to indoctrinations that have been passed on from generation to generation.

Chapter 5

Politics of Economy & Business of Politics.

Political leadership as well Business leadership plays crucial and relevant role in every countries development and progress, the world civilization can't exist without Political leadership and Business (corporate) leadership.

Both "Political and Business leadership" have mandated duty to give right guidance and ensure the safety and security of citizens and thus provide its citizen of the country opportunities or create new opportunities in Business and provide employment.

The role of political leadership is to ensure and facilitate level playing field in "Non-Partisan" manner for its citizens, the skilled labour needs the right opportunity and the unskilled workforce needs to be provide help and assistance so that they can as well live their life with dignity, the youths which are backbone of every country needs to be empowered and for that they particularly needs special attention and guidance, women empowerment is so essential to have peace in civil society.

But, does these politicians and the bosses from corporate world really leaves up to our expectation, and do they do their job in earnest? To help and to bring equality in civil society, do they in their own capacity do everything they could do for welfare and benefit of their country's citizens? And ensure that every citizens of their country get equal right and are not discriminated on the basis of "Religion or Race."

Or is it, that, these leaders be it from "politics" or from "corporate world" systematically, discriminates its own people in a very "Partisan" manner, by helping and providing job and business opportunities to select few "base on their "Race and Religion."

Well, "Yes and No," yes there are Politicians and Businessmen's who have double standards and they do systematically discriminates and promote few individuals more so not on the basis of their merit and credentials but for other reason and these other reasons are mostly all the wrong reasons, "favouritism and nepotism" first preference always to a person who's from our own fraternity or a person who can bribe his/her way "up" the ladder to success.

But, I would proudly like to say, that there are many who are overwhelmingly honest and sincere "Politicians and Businessmen's" who earnestly and with full heartedly works for the cause of common people, they provide every possible help and assistance without any fear and favour to individuals based on their intrinsic ability and on merit.

Right Ideas but Wrong Person: whether to implement "Political economic policies" or "Corporate Business Projects," at times a person with right credentials is hired to work on the project, but what happens is that the same person do not have the appropriate managerial skills and ability or the right intentions and intent to make the project that they work on a success, hence many of the government aided and business projects comprehensively fails.

In business or otherwise "compromise on skills but not on characteristic."

Does the countries which are socially progressive and economically prosperous have "Less or No" Religious or Racial "bias" or discrimination? And, does these countries provides equal opportunity and are all its citizens living with full honour and dignity?

No, not all, irrespective of whether the countries are economically prosperous or countries which are poor and impoverish, the "Caste, Region, Religious, Racial or xenophobia" related hatred crime and social injustice are "Universal," spread and deeply percolated in almost every civil societies.

Simply by writing and implementing Liberal and Secular Constitution, these is not enough, on paper the Constitution of the country we stay in maybe liberal and secular and maybe providing each of its citizens full democratic rights, but, such "Constitution Rights" proves to be inadequate of to say mere academic, in actual terms the ground reality is extremely different and excruciating, in day to day life we citizens often do not get our full democratic as well as civil rights and it's always difficult for "most people, if not all," to live in our country with full honour and dignity.

Even in the affluent industrialized and Rich Nations like "United States of America, Canada and western European countries as well, the hatred crime related to "Racial and Religious Prejudice" are rampant.

For many hundreds of years the racial divide between the "Whites and Black Africans" is ever so wide in "USA and Canada" these two "Races" never miss an opportunity to take a jibe at each other's Race, and comments Jeering Remarks.

Anti-Semitism is another problem that persist in "North-American" civil society, and worse still in the aftermath of "9-11" terrorist attack by the Islamic terrorist group "Al Qaeda" has further exasperated the problem particularly for the Muslim community leaving in "North-America," Muslim community members are suspected upon and they are stigmatised and are often accused of harming "United States" national security, there has also been news that many members of Muslim community have to at times "conceal" their religious identity to avoid any kind of backlash and hatred.

In Europe as well things are very much the same and particularly these three religious groups "the' Muslims, Jews and Hindus" are the most vulnerable to "Religious and Racial" discrimination, great degree of intolerance towards many ethnic groups is rampant.

While visiting Europe, I got an opportunity to interact with few Indians belonging to Hindu religion, and they said to me, that the colour of the skin matters a lot in Europe and many are xenophobic hence social injustice and racial discrimination is wide spread, they told me, that very often they have to listen bitter racial taunt.

Xenophobia tends to make the affected individual call everyone driving a taxi or serving a Pizza's nasty names.

Xenophobia is known to be hatred, intolerance or dislike of someone or something strange, unfamiliar. It is often perceived as incomprehensible, inconceivable, and therefore dangerous and hostile attitude towards unknown. All of us are hostile to something unknown. Unknown has been mistreated and misunderstood for ages. People hate what they do not understand. It is a tragedy that xenophobia is applicable in politics and infect the minds of normal liberal people with the superstitions and numerous clichés, stereotypes and bias. Thus, Xenophobia is often equated with nationalism.

Talking about India, well "Mumbai" is India's most progressive city and it's also a major financial hub and India's commercial capital, but, in regards to social justice "Mumbai" falters.

Like other parts of India, In Mumbai as well systematic segregation and social-injustice and discrimination is in abundant, many crafty individuals cleverly deny people permission to stay or to own a house to leave because of their ethnicity or religion they belong too, also people find it difficult to get accommodation because of their Marital status or because of their eating and drinking habits. In many of the family own Businesses there's blatant bias, these businessman always give first preferences to person of their own community, also at places of work in offices as well, the senior officers and managers will show undue favour to their favourite colleagues who most often are members of their own "caste or community."

There are basically two types of economic policy "Socialist and Capitalist" and there are three types of political systems "Socialist, Communist or Dictatorship."

To add to the "Dictatorship" theirs also "Monarch" both "Dictatorship and Monarchy" system of government is considered to be Autocratic political system in which either the Dictator or the Monarch" is supreme and wields overriding powers, often the Dictators and Monarch are accused of embezzlement and siphoning of the national wealth.

Let us understand basic of; **Communism, Socialism and Capitalism**.

Communism is an extreme form of socialism, there are many countries that have dominant Socialist Political parties, but, very few are totally communist.

Socialism is sometimes used "interchangeably with communism" but the two philosophies have some stark differences. Most notably while communist is a political system, Socialism is primarily economic system that can exist in various form under a wide range of Political System.

The failure of Communism was Total, communist countries could not even feed themselves and were always importing food.

Communism was supposed to ensure equality, but instead lead to virtual universal poverty.

The problem with socialism is that eventually you run out of other people's money (to spend).

Capitalism failure are much more subtle, capitalism is an unqualified success in producing large amount of consumer goods of good quality. There is plenty to buy in a store in capitalist country, where capitalism has failed is in ensuring that even the lowest 10 percent of the population is able to share in this table of plenty.

Capitalist country have gradually recognised this problem by providing a "social safety net."

Bottom line: Capitalism has proved to be an imperfect Solution, it works for the majority of its people, but it doesn't provide a mechanism by itself to take care of those, who fall through the cracks.

Interestingly countries where communism still exist officially but living condition are improving are the ones where Capitalist principles has been re-introduced.

China is the most obvious example of that, compare the well-being of Chinese citizen with, for example, those in North-Korea or Cuba, when Chinese loosened up on communism, their economy boomed.

Capitalist economic policy dynamics received an all new meaning and purpose in the early 1980s, by two most controversial political leaders of their time " The British Prime Minister' Mrs Margret Thatcher and President of United States of America' Mr Ronald Reagan" both these leaders with their ability inspire others to accept their new form of Capitalist economic policies.

Mrs Thatcher made the first "Bold and Courageous" move, by implementing tough economic policy into effect, Mr Reagan followed it up by dramatically freeing the "USA" economic policy allowing complete and total free trade practise, though financial rules were relax, capital markets were given prime importance, many other European governments as well followed Mrs Thatcher and Mr Reagan" and they as well adopted the new form of Capitalist economic policies.

However, these sort of new Capitalist Measures, were liked by few who immensely benefited, but large chunk peoples in from both the countries "United Kingdom and United States" severely condemn and oppose the new Capitalist economic measures taken by their respective political leaders "British Prime Minister' Margret Thatcher and USA President' Ronald Reagan" as the capitalist economic policies were considered to be stringent and radical as free and liberal trade and privatisation had made life increasingly difficult for many common people as there were many job losses and livelihood was under immense pressure, and free trade and liberal financial system had radically stirred up social inequality, the gulf between the "Rich and the Poor" was getting ever so wide.

Well the bold capitalist economic policies that were implemented in early 1980s by Thatcher and Reagan however continued to thrive despite the fact that many citizen in both continental Europe and North-America faced severe hardship.

The beginning of 1990s saw the fall of the largest Communist Block in the world The Soviet Union," many formerly communist ruled countries including Russia after the collapse of communist political system were compelled to adopt the new Political and Economic systems that were the blend of both "socialist and capitalist."

The biggest surprise was that the staunchly communist country like China relinquish it decades old "hard-core socialist" economic policies and planned new Economic reforms, they embrace the "Capitalist" economic policies and started to de-control and allowed free and liberal trade of goods and services, thereby China put into effect the more liberal western style "Capitalist" economic policies, while it still continued to be governed by its age old communist political system, So, China has proven to be perfect example, while it continues with communist political system, for business and commerce it has adopted Capitalist economic system.

The capitalist economic policies received first jolt in the year "2000," the new millennium and the "twenty-first century" had commence on rather chaotic note, the internet and technology companies which had been thriving in most part of the 1990s, the technology companies had seen their "share values" peaked to an unprecedentedly high level in the late 1990s, well as there is a saying what goes up, has to come down, and that's precisely what happened.

In the beginning of the year "2000" the so-called Dot-Com bubble burst and it burst with an phenomenon vigour, the "Stocks Prices" of all the high flying "Tech & Internet" companies collapsed, so sharp and such intense was the fall in the "Stocks-Value" of Tech & Internet" companies that many of the investors who had in the past rejoice the monetary gains they had made by betting on Tech companies "Stocks" and these same lot of Investors had built up overwhelmingly large long positions in the "Stocks" of the "Technology & Internet" companies, many among these Investors overnight became impecunious because of the sharp fall in the Stock Value of the "Technology & Internet" companies, this was the first setback the Capitalist economic policies had received, and this crisis plunge the global economy into recession.

The world was yet reeling with the "Dot-Com" bubble burst and the economy was still in severe recession, the worse tragedy took place, when the Islamic terrorist the "Al Qaeda" led by its then chief "Osama Bin Laden" plotted and launched on "11.09.2001" (09-11) a major terror attack right in the heart of America's central business district, by blasting two huge tower buildings in New-York, this terror attack unnerved not just the United States of America but the whole world, which led to Two wars first USA attacked Afghanistan and then attacked Iraq to dislodge "Saddam" from power.

The year 2008 had an evil in store for the world, the Capitalist economy faltered, the collapse of big investment bank and brokerage house "The' Lehman Brothers," The notorious "Lehman Brother" scam and its fall resulted in sharp global financial meltdown.

The two major financial crisis first the so-called "Dot-Com" bubble burst than more horrendous collapse of the entire financial systems, nearly every large

USA's and European banks suffered and failed to large extent in meeting and honouring their financial commitments of their customers and clients, and the governments of all major countries had to step in to bail out their faltering banking system by doling out unprecedented amount of hard cash, and all these cash given by the governments to their banks were by the way of printing currency notes, the central banks of most countries made the printing press work overtime to print currency notes.

The 2008 financial meltdown cause primarily by the collapse of an investment Bank the "Lehman Brothers," compelled the staunch Capitalist Economies of the world like the "United States of America and European union countries" to adopt the much less glamorous and exciting "Socialist economic system" the USA and European union under tremendous pressure from within and from its own people and trade unions to safeguard the interest of their domestic industry and to save jobs as well as to create new jobs for its citizens.

These capitalist countries made compelling changes in their otherwise liberal trade policy, by becoming more protectionist, many liberal trade and corporate laws were withdrawn, and more stringent trade policy was drafted and put into effect, many generous benefits and incentives were rendered to corporates that creates job and starts business in their own countries and those corporates were severely disincentive who took the American or European jobs away from home and particularly to Asian countries.

There is a well-known saying about capitalism economic system which is: that capitalism makes "Rich Richer and Poor Poorer," here I would also like to add what I've observed, the other side of the story of capitalism is, few people rise from "Rags to Rich and on flip side Riches to Rags." Yes, capitalism economic system makes people more voracious cupid and selfish. In capitalism the story is all about creating cash liquidity. The political administration managing capitalism simply gives standing instruction to their respective country's central bank governors to flush the money market with unprecedented amount of cash liquidity, and to ensure wealth is created by those brave hearts and crafty individuals who are willing to take risk by keeping the capital and commodity markets in good health.

Whether socialist or capitalist ever since the beginning of the Twenty-first century the prime and principle focus of the politicians from across the demographics has become is to keep the capital markets buoyant, simply by printing unprecedented amount of currency notes and flooding the money markets with Hard-currency notes, these politicians and economist have found the easiest and simplest way of tackling the most challenging and difficult economic and social problem.

Rather than applying minds thinking of innovative and creative ideas, to find more human way of boosting economy and implementing social reforms to ensure peace and security in civil society, "Arab Spring" conflict that began in the year 2011 and which has devastated not only the Arab and Islamic world but the whole world is also according to some political experts the fall-out of bad and reckless economic policy and lack of transparency in functioning of political system.

Think big - Dream big: cutting across lines and in many countries and sections of societies, encourage by governments manoeuvre, people from all strata even the "Shoe-polish boys, Taxi-drivers and Restaurant waiters" have started to dabble with their hard earn cash in Stock markets. Life after all is all about living on razors edge, Risk is rewarding but reckless Risk taking can decimate a person's life for ever.

When "passion is immense nothing else matters."

Over the past many years and decades be it socialist or capitalist economic policy system both these types of economic policies have brought in huge progress and prosperity in households in many countries, the perfect examples are that increasing numbers of people in formerly socialist and communist countries like "China, Russia and India" have become millionaires and billionaires.

The living standard of many around the globe may have got upgraded. But the significant economic prosperity has cause huge and emphatic ecological disaster. Yes, the global weather condition is by the day becoming more and more uncertain and erratic, uncertain times have become even more uncertain as for weather is concern, which is increasingly making the survival of humans on this planet uncertain.

As said before, the benefit is not in discussing your ideas and thoughts with others but the fruits are in executing your ideas, so, whenever the change is made, whether social reforms or political reforms the transformation is always going to be difficult, particularly when the political leadership have to implement new economic reforms, apparently economic reforms the most difficult reform to execute as its always very difficult for the policy makers and the political leadership to appease every section of the society, and because whenever there is a major changes made in economic policies of a country, it brings a lot of benefit to only certain class of the society, but the other section of the society that finds themselves at disadvantage and feels insecure about their future, that's when they resent against their government, which often results in potential civilian unrest in the country, in history you will find many examples, wherein the countries have plunged into civil war, due to hasty or reckless implementation of political and economic reform policies.

One of the prime reason for the unrest in civil society in many European countries after World-War 1, was that out of desperation many countries had to make radical changes to its political systems and radically reform its economic policies, which had caused lots of hardship to many European people and apparently among many reasons the economic hardship was also one of the main reason for the start of World-War 2.

The Contemporary Technology apparently doesn't create much jobs, but on the contrary the advent of many new technologies takeaway or dilutes existing job opportunities.

The Americans and the British have prejudice against Indians and Chinese, the Americans and European are outrageous and often accuses, that the Indians and the Chinese to have taken away many of their jobs and business opportunities, the manufacturing jobs have been taken away by the Chinese and service sector jobs by the Indians.

Well, the dynamics are changing further, now, the manufacturing cost in China is rising as well, the labour in China is no longer cheap, hence the Chinese "Corporates" are revising and evolving new strategy to remain competitive, the Chinese manufactures have started outsourcing some of their manufacturing work to the countries which are even more cost competitive, for example; many Chinese manufacturers now outsource most their manufacturing work to countries like Pakistan and Bangladesh and even from Africa, now in future, will it happen? That, after few years like "Americans and the Europeans" the Chinese as well will have racial prejudice or otherwise against the Bangladeshis or Pakistanis or Africans for stealing their jobs and business opportunities away from them.

Now, desperate time calls for desperate measures, keeping commercial interest in mind the businesses and business managers are always looking for cost effectiveness and efficiencies as well as value for money opportunity, to make their business successful one has to be astute and cunning, business can't be done with emotions and patriotism, hence these large or small size company and every corporate houses keep on churning their business plans, as the corporates have to also have to keep in mind the interest of its stock-holders, because the stock-holders always keep exerting pressure on the management to enhance the value of their stock, by making more profit.

The people of Black African "Race" bemoan the most, and rightly so, because the people of African origin experiences the most "social injustice" maximum number of "racial abuses" most number of hatred crimes are committed against the Black Africans and various kind of discriminations the Black Africans suffers in their life time.

Yes, rightly so, the Black people of African origin have suffered the most "racial abuses" and one of the paramount reason could be because many Black Africans are desperately poor and socio-culturally backwards and less academically qualified.

But the Black Africans need to do some serious introspection about their plight and not simply blame the others, they need to find out whether they have failed themselves, could they would they have been better off if they had not been so feeble and have not allowed the invaders into their countries to take undue advantage of the natural resources that they have of which they were and are the sole owners.

Nature has blessed the African continent with vast amount of natural resources like mines and minerals and hydrocarbon as well as most part of African land is fertile and suitable to grow the best quality crops.

Then, what happen? Why have the black Africans not taken advantage of their own resources which is available in abundant? "Tear the earth and take out the wealth that is yours," but no, the Africans made a major strategic mistakes and worse still the corrupt politics and politicians simply added to the woes of Africans, when the industrial revolution begin in Europe, Africa became the favourite hunting ground for the Europeans to source the desperately needed raw material to manufacture goods and material.

First the Europeans and then later the Americans of the European descent, started visiting Africa and started taking away the raw minerals "in raw form" like "Copper, Zinc, Aluminium, Gold, Silver and Diamonds" to their countries and the raw minerals were used as raw material to manufacture the high end value added goods thereby the by taking away the raw minerals and high value agriculture crops like "Cocoa, Vanilla and Tobacco, and using it to manufacture high priced high end value added goods and materials, this is how the American corporates as well as European corporates houses were able to create jobs in their own countries and more importantly these corporates were able to create better job and business opportunities in their countries and thereby boosting the standard of living of their citizens, these is how the American and the European companies simply by sourcing the raw material from African countries have thrived and made trillions of dollars in profit for the past hundreds of years.

And now in the "twenty-first" century the Chinese are trying to do to Africa what the Europeans and the American governments and corporates have done for hundreds of years, now it's the Chinese government and its corporates are sourcing rich Africans minerals and agriculture crops and making huge profit out of it by adding value to the raw material they source from Africa as well they are creating more job and business opportunity in their own country.

Like the Europeans and Americans the Chinese as well, in return as a gesture of goodwill to make the Africans bit happy and satisfied, they built few hospitals and playgrounds and develop few thousand miles long roads and highways.

The Africans would be well advised that they first stop taking any kind of generous donation and goodwill gesture from other donor countries, if Africans wants to improve their standard of living, alleviate poverty and upgrade socio-cultural status then they will have to stop other countries from sourcing raw material from their country and instead the Africans will have to start setting up "fully integrated" manufacturing units in their own country, by adding value to the raw material which is available in abundant in their own country and have fully geared and entrenched manufacturing facility, it will create millions of new job for the Africans and raise their standard of living.

Economic inequality is essential to drive growth and progress, rewarding those with talent and skills, and the ambition to innovate and take entrepreneurial risks. However, the extreme levels of wealth concentration occurring today threatens to exclude hundreds of millions of people from realizing the benefits of their talent and hard work.

Extreme economic inequality is damaging and worrying for many reasons, it is morally questionable, it can have negative impacts on economic growth and poverty reduction, and it can multiply social problems. It compounds other inequalities, such as those between women and men.

The present crisis is not just a crisis of the growing scarcity of natural resources and services. It fundamentally is the crisis of a type of civilization that has put the human being as the "lord and master" of Nature (Desecrate). In this civilization, nature has neither spirit nor purpose, and therefore, humans can do what they want with her.

In the countries most affected by the consequences of the economic crisis, there has been an increase in the appeal of extremist parties that are rooted in a profound hostility to ethnic, religious and cultural diversity. Their aggressive rhetoric often fuels intolerance towards ethnic or religious minorities by insinuating they are a danger to national identity or even national security, which can lead to a proliferation of hate crimes and racist attacks.

Chapter 6

Discrimination and prejudice against women,

Women deserve to be treated as equals to men. It would appear to be an obvious right, and yet throughout history women have been oppressed by men–they have not had the same employment opportunities, educational opportunities, or even the right to vote. Indeed women have been treated like second class citizens, and still are in many countries, where the principles behind feminism are not widely accepted.

Women are as intrinsically worthwhile as men on the basis that there are no difference between men and women. Yet this is patently untrue. As it turns out, while the differences don't mean that women or men are better than one another, it is in these differences that the reasons for men's oppression of women can be found.

High poverty rates among women are caused by discriminatory policies, practices and opinions "such as labour market restrictions, lower wages for women, lack of equal education opportunities, substandard healthcare for women etc."

Where there is a clear economic or cultural preference for sons, the misuse of "pregnancy diagnostic tools" can facilitate female feticide. This means that in parts of the world, like China and India, parents will abort their child or put the child up for adoption on the basis that it's a girl.

Millions of women throughout the world live in conditions in which they are deprived of their basic human rights for no other reason than their gender.

When Jihadists wage their war, it is often the women that suffers the most. Approximately 10,000 women die in honour killings every year, which the Islamic extremists declare imperative.

Female abuse is a common phenomenon that takes shape in several forms in societies. However this phenomenon tends to be extreme in certain communities, where women are mercilessly "Battered" by males of their household.

The magnitude of the problem of the Battered women is not only the result of the damage these women go through during and after being battered, but also the result of secrecy that they are forced to keep out of fear that if they divulge their sufferings they will bring dishonour to themselves and their families.

The reasons that stand behind women "Battering" are many, some men beat women because they feel physically strong. Ironically this physical superiority is only displayed over females, almost never over other "Males."

Its widely perceived and believed that there is no document in the world that states that the "Male" is in anyway better than female, and such behaviour only reveals perverted traditions and Male insecurity.

Attitudes toward women and socially approved roles for women are another set of markers for a culture. Worldwide, women are playing more important roles in the practice of public relations. Consequently, the evolving role of women is strongly affecting the evolving role of public relations in society.

The vastly more daunting task to expand women's participation in society will be to dismantle centuries-old discrimination.

On their part, The Men like to be superior and like to take total control over women, men's don't like aggressive girls, men likes to be complimented, men likes when a girl compliments him for his intelligence or for his body looks.

But on the flip side, Are the Men's solely responsible for all of women plight and their agony?

Agreed that women gender have been discriminated for as long as recorded history, but, is it right for women to squarely put the blame on Male gender for all their misery?

There are other burning issues concerning women, which as well are issues of immense significant and one must take these into consideration as well.

So, how much actually are women supportive for the cause of women?

Now, this is not my own thought, but this is an observation of many and I've heard this comments from many women themselves, that, "Women are the biggest enemies of women."

At times a woman becomes a big stumbling block for the progress of other women.

Some Women who are religious and socio-culturally conservative envy's the freedom of and often smear about and belittle the dignity of those women who are liberal and secular in their belief.

Forget the sisterhood. Women are in it for themselves — and will clamber over female colleagues to get to the top. Women will also push themselves much harder than men because they feel they need to be at their desks to prove they're working hard. The support for women's social, economic and professional achievements worldwide, when it comes down to a local, everyday level, women can be their own worst enemies.

Girls can be mean to other girls, but it is adult women who vie to destroy each other, Secret social battles are waged, in many cases, by the very same women singing the praises of girl power, feminism, and female friendship in their lives.

The lower level of respect appearing to be shown by women towards women is worthy of further exploration and discussion as this perception may be limiting the extent to which gender issues are taken seriously in the working world.

Achieving the development goals is an urgent necessity if the world is to be a safe place to live, Women needs to be educated and given tool of knowledge and awareness to open their eyes to their rights.

Chapter 7

The modern civilization of technology has filled everything with its devices, and has been able to penetrate to the heart of the matter, of life and of the universe. Everything comes wrapped in the aura of "progress," a sort of recuperation of the paradise that was lost some time before, but is now rebuilt and offered to all.

The glorious vision began to crumble in the twentieth century with the two world wars and other colonial wars that produced 200 million victims. The greatest terrorist act of the history was perpetrated when the US army launched the atomic bombs against Japan, killing thousands of people and destroying Nature. This gave humanity a shock from which it has not yet recovered. With the atomic, biological and chemical weapons built afterwards, we have come to realize that we do not need to be God to make the Apocalypse a reality.

Rising inequality and ever so growing income gap between the rich and poor, almost half of the world's wealth is now owned by just one percent of the population, Massive concentration of economic resources in the hands of fewer people presents a significant threat to inclusive political and economic systems. Instead of moving forward together, people are increasingly separated by economic and political power, inevitably heightening social tensions and increasing the risk of civil society breakdown.

Favouritism, cronyism, and nepotism all interfere with fairness because they give undue advantage to someone who does not necessarily merit this treatment. In the public sphere, favouritism, cronyism, and nepotism also undermine the common good. When someone is granted a position because of connections rather than because he or she has the best credentials and experience, the service that the person renders to the public may be inferior.

Basically favouritism is just what it sounds like, it's favouring a person not because he or she is doing the best job but rather because of some extraneous feature-membership in a favoured group, personal likes and dislikes, etc. Favouritism can be demonstrated in hiring, honouring, or awarding contracts. A related idea is patronage, giving public service jobs to those who may have helped elect the person who has the power of appointment.

Cronyism is a more specific form of favouritism, referring to partiality towards friends and associates. As the old saying goes, "It's not what you know but who you know," or, as blogger Danny Ferguson puts it, "It's not what you don't know, it's who your college roommate knows." Cronyism occurs within a network of insiders-the "good ol' boys," who confer favours on one another.

Nepotism is an even narrower form of favouritism. Coming from the Italian word for nephew, it covers favouritism to members of the family. Both nepotism and cronyism are often at work when political parties recruit candidates for public office.

Probably the biggest dilemma presented by favouritism is that, under various other names, few people see it as a problem. Connections, networking, family-ties, we have all drawn on these sources of support in job hunting. So, what's the problem? The first issue is competence. For high level positions, an executive should hire experienced, qualified and skilled candidates, but historically, it's more likely for someone's past friend from work or political appointment ally to be slipped into a job for which she/he is not qualified or there are more qualified candidates.

The solutions are their but the intent is not there in we humans to resolve all the relevant issues amicably, basically people have forgot the essence of love.

Here I would like add couple of interesting paragraphs from the bestselling Book "**Rape: Weapon of War and Mass Destruction**," have a listen; "This advice is "Not" for "weak hearted" risk averse people, but, for those "Brave-hearts" who believe in taking that odd Risk in life, to achieve our goals in life just do not bother yourself thinking, simply move ahead with your decision that you think will potentially shape-up your future so take step forward and make your life the best experience, move on do not to hesitate and worry about any types of "Legal Implication or Social Consequences," if Conventional methods fails, there is no harm in trying Un-Conventional methods, but don't give up without trying, just move ahead and execute your ideas, bother about implementing your ideas don't simply waste time contemplating and discussing your thoughts, motivate yourself, get inspire by this famous saying "luck favours the brave," as most often its seen, the goal of keeping our head float above water only ends up sinking us, live life not simply to survive but to thrive.

Very important to note: Always be **Assertive**, Never ever be **Aggressive**; your assertiveness will send positive signal to your Clients/Customers and to your business and professional competitors and Rivals, whereas being aggressive will turn your friends and peer's into foe, and will make your professional and business rivals your most bitter enemy. Always be in the habit of fulfilling your commitments even at the cost of you suffering personal loss or no matter how big sacrifice you have to make. Not fulfilling commitments may possibly not harm us but it significantly harms the whole mankind, as people who suffers from betrayal losses faith in humanity."..........

I would like to add couple of more paragraphs from the Book "**Arab Spring Women's Nightmare**," "Let's elaborate little more by going into details of the issue so as to understand things from ground level perspective, as in, modern times most countries particularly the most developed nations economies are not creating those lucrative high paying white collar jobs, funds are not so easily available for youths (men and women) to start their own business, so than, what is the solution for new young generation? How will the new generation youth survive? Everybody crave for better standard of living high quality life styles, well every new generations have to learn to cope with and learn to deal with and accept the challenges the circumstances throws at them. The working class and youths will have to become more innovative and creative in their thinking, they will have to think of new professional and business ideas and dare to execute those ideas.

So, how do people become innovative and creative? Is good quality of academic qualification and higher qualification degrees will help new generation boys and girls become creative and intelligent, the answer is "No" not really, good quality academic qualification helps person to only some extent, because it is one thing to be academically qualified and another thing to be intellectually brilliant, yes it is always nice to have quality and quantity of academic qualification, but, friends the ground level reality of life is a whole lot different from what you learn in Text Books in schools, colleges and universities, same as how the "Real life is different from Reel life that we see in film cinema." So, how does a person develops good creative and innovative skills to succeed professionally or starts his/her business with good ideas and thrive, yes, to succeed in life, what's particularly important is to develop good **Critical Thinking Skills,** only those individuals who are steadfast **Determined** can develop good **Critical Thinking Skills,** good critical thinking skills makes a person intellectually brilliant in true sense, helps develop Brain which ultimately helps and provides person/persons better perspective of life, with good critical thinking skills those particular individuals become more and more innovative and creative and strong enough to accept any challenges which life will throws at them.".........

There are many questions human asks of themselves: Why am I here? What is my origin and purpose? What does it mean to be human? Who and what am I? What is my end? These are certainly very ancient questions that, both with every new generation and repeatedly within each generation, rise to the surface of the human mind. The pressing question that follows is, where are the answers?

Given the daunting array of proposed solutions to questions about human, some insist that there are no answers: the truth about who the human is, it will forever remain elusive.

Defeat teaches us many lessons, provided we are ready to learn from our past mistakes, victory at times makes person/persons complacent, hence for those who feel defeated should try to recoup and keep the disappointment of defeat at bay energise themselves and vehemently move ahead in life to accept the next challenges, never run away from accepting challenges.

Discussion is always better than argument, because argument is to find who is right, Discussion is to find out what is right.

Your job is not to judge, your job is not to figure out if someone deserves something, your job is to lift the fallen, to restore the broken, and to heal the hurting.

18815357R00040

Printed in Great Britain
by Amazon